Th

Ruzbihan Baqli

The Unveiling of Secrets
Diary of a Sufi Master

Translated by Carl W. Ernst

Parvardigar Press

The Unveiling of Secrets was designed and composed in Adobe Garamond by
Kachergis Book Design, Pittsboro, North Carolina. It was printed on 60-pound
Writers Natural and bound by McNaughton & Gunn, Inc., Saline, Michigan.

Printed and bound in the United States of America

The paper used in this publication meets the minimum requirements of the Ameri-
can National Standard for Information Science—Permanence of Paper for Printed
Library Materials, ANSI Z39.48-1984

The illustration shown in detail on the cover and in full on the title page is from
the *Mi'raj Nameh* (Supplement Turc 190, fol. 49v) and is reproduced by permission
of the Bibliothèque Nationale, Paris.

PUBLISHER'S CATALOGING IN PUBLICATION
Baqli, Ruzbihan ibn Abi al-Nasr, d. 1209 or 10.
    [Kashf al-asrar. English]
    The unveiling of secrets : diary of a Sufi master / Ruzbihan Baqli ; translat-
ed by Carl W. Ernst.
        p.   cm.
    Includes bibliographical references and indexes.
    Preassigned LCCN : 96-72579
    ISBN 0-9644362-1-3
    1. Baqli, Ruzbihan ibn Abi al-Nasr, d. 1209 or 10—Diaries.   2. Sufism—
Biography.   3. Sufism.   4. Mysticism.   I. Ernst, Carl W., 1950-   II. Title.
III. Title : Ruzbihan Baqli.
    BP80.B262.E7   1997   297'.4'092
                                                    QBI97-40079

هو الحق

In the early twelfth century, a falcon named Ruzbihan was born in Pasa near Shiraz. He soared so high in the atmosphere of God's essence that he surpassed his predecessors. If in terms of the path we call Junayd the Monarch of the Sufism of Knowledge, then we must call Ruzbihan the Prophet of the Sufism of Love. It is obvious that the difference between the experience of love and the exercise of reason is like that between heaven and earth. The great masters of Khurasan planted the seed of the Sufism of Love. Rabiᶜa, Hallaj, Shibli, and others watered it, till it grew into a tree, which came to bear fruit through Ruzbihan's spiritual aspiration.

Ruzbihan's statements about Sufism were so profound and to the point that whatever was said after him served as no more than footnotes to what he had said. Because his statements were above the level of understanding of most Sufis, he was known as the "Ecstatic Speaker *(shattah)* of Fars." One must read the writings of this lover of God to be launched into the highest realms and the farthest reaches of his vision. One who reads his works will have washed away the libraries of all faiths.

Dr. Javad Nurbakhsh
London, 3 July 1996

Contents

Preface

The study of Sufism, or Islamic mysticism, is a subject that is still very little known in the West.[1] The poetry of the great Persian Sufi Jalaluddin Rumi is now becoming extremely popular in English versions, but there are scores of major Sufis whose names are still hardly known in Europe and America. One of these Sufis was Ruzbihan Baqli (d. 1209), a remarkable mystic who lived in Shiraz. In his own day, and for several centuries afterward, Ruzbihan was known throughout the Middle East and India as one of the most profound authors in the Sufi tradition. The poet Hafiz (d. 1389) was apparently a member of the Sufi order founded by Ruzbihan's family. Ruzbihan's renown faded, however, so that by the turn of the century his name had become almost forgotten in his home country, and his tomb in Shiraz had become a ruin. In recent years his writings have been rediscovered by a small group of modern scholars in Iran, India, Turkey, and Europe; a number of his Arabic and Persian writings have been published, and in 1972 the Iranian Department of Antiquities restored his tomb (which I had the privilege of visiting in 1996). I recently published an overview of Ruzbihan's life and teachings, focusing on his visionary diary, *The Unveiling of Secrets,* and two biographies of him written by his descendants.[2] Readers of early drafts of that book were so struck by the excerpts from *The Unveiling of Secrets* that they per-

1. For a survey of the subject, see Carl W. Ernst, *The Shambhala Guide to Sufism* (Boston: Shambhala, 1997).
2. Carl W. Ernst, *Ruzbihan Baqli: Mystical Experience and the Rhetoric of Sainthood in Persian Sufism,* Curzon Sufi Series (London: Curzon Press, 1996).

suaded me to produce this translation, the first complete book by Ruzbihan to be rendered into English. Those who are interested in more complete information are referred to that study, *Ruzbihan Baqli,* for full details about his biography and his writings; the introductory remarks that follow are a much abbreviated account of what has been set forth there.

The Unveiling of Secrets is one of the most powerful documents in the history of mysticism. Unlike most Sufi writings, it is written in the first person, as Ruzbihan records his visionary encounters with God, the angels, the prophets, and the Sufi saints. Ruzbihan began writing the book in 1181, when he was fifty-five years old, starting out with an autobiographical account of his spiritual experiences, beginning in early childhood in the Persian town of Pasa. At the age of fifteen, Ruzbihan was overwhelmed by an experience that caused him to abandon his vegetable shop (from which his surname, Baqli, "the grocer," is derived). After wandering in the desert for over a year, he joined the Sufis for years of meditative discipline, finally settling in the city of Shiraz; his followers (many of whom belonged to the stone masons' guild) built a hospice or lodge for him there in 1165. Unlike many mystical authors, Ruzbihan refers repeatedly to members of his family, revealing his pain at the death of a favorite wife, and his pleas for divine assistance when his son raged with fever during a widespread plague. Otherwise Ruzbihan says little about the outward events of his life, and he only makes passing reference to the Turkish princes who ruled Shiraz at the time. Although Ruzbihan records visionary encounters with the great Sufis of previous years, he mentions by name only one of his Sufi contemporaries, a fellow novice with whom he practiced devotional exercises.

Since the original text is devoid of any internal divisions or punctuation, I have with a certain amount of arbitrariness divided the text into a total of 210 sections; each section has been given a title indicative of its contents. The autobiographical memoir (Part

One) only takes up about one-fifth of *The Unveiling of Secrets*. Because of its sequential character, this portion can be divided into several sections devoted to particular themes. At that point, the character of the narration changes, as the remainder of the book (Part Two) becomes something like an ongoing diary, evidently maintained for eight years until 1189. The contents of the diary cover a dazzling array of themes, with sequences observable only in an extended series of visions from the month of Ramadan (☸ 128–159), and in the concluding passages which allude to a plague epidemic in Shiraz (☸ 200–209; the date 1189 is mentioned in ☸ 206). The language of the book is Arabic, which was the primary language of Sufism before the Mongol conquests of the thirteenth century (of the more than forty writings credited to Ruzbihan, less than one-fourth are known to have been written in Persian). Writing at the request of an unnamed intimate disciple, Ruzbihan wrote in a prose of direct, emotional intensity. As one Iranian scholar has observed, "His speech is like a rose that flutters apart once grasped in the hand, or like an alchemical substance that turns into vapor when barely heated. His language is the language of perceptions; he praises the beautiful and beauty, and he loves them both."[3]

Ruzbihan's mysticism is profoundly Islamic. He was the author of one of the most important commentaries on the Qurʾan, so it is not surprising to see that the language of his diary is saturated with references to the Qurʾan; it is quoted dozens of times. He also frequently cites the mystical sayings of the Prophet Muhammad. Ruzbihan's technical vocabulary for mystical experience is highly developed, and one of the challenges of producing this translation has been to employ English equivalents that would at least suggest the power and precision of the Arabic terms. The primary category

3. Muhammad Muʿin, in *Le Jasmin des Fidèles d'amour, Kitâb-e ʿAbhar al-ʿâshiqîn,* ed. Henry Corbin and Muhammad Muʿin, Bibliothéque Iranienne, 8 (Tehran: Intisharat-i Manuchihri, 1365/1981), Introduction, p. 100.

for him in the diary is vision, as most of the episodes begin with the phrase, "Then I saw . . ." He uses the language of Islamic theology to describe the essence, attributes, and actions of God. He describes the levels of existence in terms of the angelic realm, the hidden realm, the realm of might, and the kingdom. God, often simply called "the Truth," reveals himself to Ruzbihan through the modes of manifestation and appearance, in the forms of greatness, magnificence, glory, splendor, power, loveliness, majesty, and beauty.

Moments of ecstasy stretch into endless horizons of what he calls pre-eternity, eternity, and post-eternity. These mystical experiences, broadly classified into the states and stations known to many Sufi authors, are refined in his treatment into a subtle phenomenology. The rare barren hours where God does not reveal himself are followed by constriction of the heart. He implores God for new visions in midnight vigils; he is reduced to tears, sighs, cries, and shouts. When God does unveil his divine qualities, Ruzbihan feels expansive, astonished, full of longing and love. He also feels familiar, intimate, and so close to God that his ego is annihilated and divine qualities emerge in the human. The fundamental metaphor in the diary is the dynamic of veiling and unveiling. What is unveiled? It is the inner conscience, the secret *(sirr)* within the heart that is close to God. As the Prophet Muhammad said, God has veiled himself in seventy thousand veils of light. The process of union with God is first experienced as a progressive unveiling of those luminous barriers. Yet the essence of divinity is beyond imagination and conception; human nature is incapable of directly experiencing God in his infinity. God's mercy is so ample, however, that he makes himself visible to his lovers by clothing himself in forms, which are the forms of divinity. Thus it is that Ruzbihan sees God appear to him, in human form, on an almost daily basis.

Those who are acquainted with standard presentations of Islamic theology may ask at this point: how is it possible to reconcile these visions of God with the well-known Islamic rejection of anthropomorphism? To this question let it first of all be said that the issue of God's incomparability is a highly complex one in Islamic thought, for it is impossible to conceive of a God that is totally unlike humanity. When the Qurʾan describes the hand of God, the face of God, etc., Muslim thinkers have wavered between understanding these expressions as pure metaphor, and accepting them as literally true, without asking how. Islamic theology typically distinguishes the unknowable, transcendent essence of God from the primary divine attributes (knowledge, power, life, hearing, seeing, speech, and will), which are comprehensible by analogy to human characteristics; the divine actions are the means by which these attributes interact with creation. The full range of divine attributes is commonly equated with the ninety-nine names of God mentioned in the Qurʾan, which are further divided into the attributes of grace and wrath. The repetition and remembrance *(dhikr)* of these names of God in fact constitutes one of the central spiritual practices of Sufism. Ruzbihan is fully aware of the tension between idolatrous comparison of God to a created human being (anthropomorphism) and the overly abstract stripping away of all human qualities from God (abstractionism). The following vision is a good example of the way Ruzbihan struggles to explain how the power of divine transcendence coexists with the forms of divine manifestation.

> After midnight I saw him, the Transcendent One, as though he appeared in a thousand kinds of beauty, among which I saw a glory of lofty likeness, "and he has the loftiest likeness [in the heavens and the earth,] and he is the mighty, the commanding" [Qurʾan 30:27]. It was as though he were like the glory of the red rose, and this is a likeness. But God forbid that he have a likeness! "There is no likeness unto him" [Qurʾan 42:11]. Yet I cannot describe except by an expression, and this description is

from the perspective of my weakness and incapacity and my lack of comprehension of the qualities of eternity. In the river bed of pre-eternity there are deserts and wastelands in which dwell the snakes of wrath. If one of then opened its mouth, none of creation or time would escape. Beware the one who describes the pre-eternal Lord, for in the oceans of his oneness all spirits and consciences are drowned, and they vanish in the sublimities of his greatness and might (❀ 87).

What makes Ruzbihan's visions especially striking is his ability to analyze them in terms of the sophisticated vocabularies of Sufism and Islamic theology. God's wrath is correlated with transcendence and the attributes of majesty, greatness, and might, which annihilate the finite ego, while his grace manifests itself in the attributes of beauty, mercy, and love, which fill the human with divine presence. According to the Sufis, these qualities of God cannot be grasped by ordinary knowledge; they can only be attained by mystical knowledge.

Ruzbihan describes his visions in forms of intense, rarefied beauty, creating a mine of images successfully quarried by generations of later poets. He undergoes initiation experiences that have cosmic ramifications, as when a pair of white-robed shaykhs feed him with oil made from "the milk of the Little Bear" (the pole star constellation, an allusion to the "pole" as the head of the hierarchy of saints). God looks down upon him from the "windows of heaven" in the stars. In visions filled with imperial symbolism, God proclaims that Ruzbihan is his "chief representative" *(khalifa)* on earth. Ruzbihan receives special initiations from figures such as the immortal prophet Khidr, and the mysterious saints called "Substitutes." He sees the angels in forms simultaneously beautiful and terrible, with long hair like women but at the same time armed like Turkish soldiers. The prophets, from Adam to Moses and Muhammad, encounter Ruzbihan in transcendental landscapes of infinite deserts and endless oceans, sometimes even in an ocean of wine. The great Sufi saints of the past witness scenes of intimacy and intoxication in which God showers Ruzbihan with roses and calls him his beloved. He drinks wine with the prophets, wine that has become in Sufi imagery a symbol of intoxication with divine love, rather than the earthly drink forbidden in Islamic law. Although it is impossible to duplicate the rhythmic power and dense texture of Ruzbihan's Arabic prose in translation, I have tried to retain a sense of the original energy and enthusiasm in this English version.

The imagery of Ruzbihan's visions belongs to that class of mystical experience associated with ascension to the divine presence. Although the ascension of the soul through the heavens is documented in many Mediterranean and Middle Eastern traditions, in Sufism this complex of images is associated above all with the ascension of the Prophet Muhammad. His role in *The Unveiling of Secrets* is crucial in many ways, but the symbolism of ascension is the most important structure underlying Ruzbihan's visions. The Prophet's ascension became the model of mystical experience in Sufism. It is particularly in the figure of the great Persian Sufi Abu Yazid al-Bistami that one can find an elaborate internal recapitulation of the Prophet's journey to the divine presence. Many of the motifs from Abu Yazid's ascension echo again in the visions of Ruzbihan.

This book aims to introduce to a wider audience one of the most powerful voices in the Sufi tradition. Ruzbihan is well known far beyond his native Persia; Sufis from North Africa, Central Asia, and India knew him as *al-shaykh al-shattah,* "The Master of Ecstatic Speech." Popular stories of his love and passion have been told by authors such as Ibn ʿArabi and ʿIraqi, but his actual writings on mystical love are far more potent. Ruzbihan may be compared with St. Augustine and Hildegard of Bingen among the Christian mystics. Like Augustine, Ruzbihan was a scriptural commentator and a skilled orator, having preached twice weekly in the mosque of Shiraz for many years. Like Hildegard, he was the recipient of intense visions of God refracted through the forms of nature. To these qualities Ruzbihan added a poetic intensity and luminous ecstasy that would be hard to match in any tradition. As he remarked, "Not a day or night has gone by me, except as God wished, from the time of my maturity until now, when I am fifty-five years old, without an unveiling of the hidden world" (⊕ 56).

The translation is based on the two known complete manuscripts of the Arabic text, one from the library attached to the shrine of Imam Reza in Mashhad, Iran, and the other from the collection of Louis Massignon in Paris. I am grateful to Dr. Amir Moezzi, Professor James Morris, Professor Herbert Mason, and Dr. Daniel Massignon for their generosity in making copies of these manuscripts available to me. The abridged version of the text known from manuscripts in Turkey (published by Nazif Hoca) and Iraq (edited by Paul Nwyia) is of less importance, but it has also been consulted. Dr. Javad Nurbakhsh, who has previously edited several Persian texts by and about Ruzbihan, plans to edit and publish the Arabic text of *The Unveiling of Secrets* with a modern Persian translation in the near future. In revising my translation, I have been immensely aided by having access to the recently published French version of *The Unveiling of Secrets* by my colleague Dr. Paul Ballanfat.[4] Readers interested in the slight variations between the copies may refer to the notes in Ballanfat's excellent translation.

The version presented here does not presuppose any particular knowledge of Sufism or of Islamic history. It is addressed to anyone who is interested in mystical experience and the passionate struggle to put it into words. The translation is designed to be intelligible in itself, without footnotes, so occasional amplifications of the text have been added in brackets. In case the reader wishes to know

4. Rûzbehân al-Baqlî al-Shîrâzî, *Le Dévoilement des secrets et les apparitions des lumières, Journal spirituel du maître de Shîrâz,* trans. Paul Ballanfat (Paris: Éditions du Seuil, 1996).

more, several indices have been included as appendices: (1) an index of passages from Ruzbihan's *The Unveiling of Secrets* that are discussed in my book *Ruzbihan Baqli: Mystical Experience and the Rhetoric of Sainthood in Persian Sufism* (the section numbering is the same in both books), (2) an index of Qurʾanic passages and sayings of the Prophet Muhammad quoted by Ruzbihan, and (3) a combined index and glossary of names and terms. These tools make it possible to clarify the themes that Ruzbihan weaves together in his narrative. Some readers may wish simply to start at the beginning and read through to the end. This approach will provide a cumulative sense of the range of experiences and images that Ruzbihan commands. Those who wish to read more selectively might wish to read first the parts of the autobiographical memoir that concern Ruzbihan's early life (✿ 7–13) and his first visions of initiations (✿ 14–40) to get a sense of the context for his visions; the reader should be aware that in the first few sections (✿ 1–3), Ruzbihan provides a formal introduction that exhibits all the rhetorical density of Arabic rhyming prose. Or one can simply browse at random until a striking passage pops out, or "manifests itself" as Ruzbihan would say. I first began reading Ruzbihan some twenty years ago. From the first, he captivated me with his rich and passionate imagery, and his eloquent, rhyming balance. I envy the readers of this book, who will experience the shock of recognition that comes when one reads a truly great author for the first time.

In translating, I have struggled between literal consistency and the demands of idiomatic English; I am only too aware of how far it falls short of the ideal. Scholars often seek literal accuracy in translation, consistently using a single English word to render a foreign word. This technique is really useful only as a first approximation, as an aid for those who wish to study the original text. But if a wider audience is to be reached, the real challenge for the translator is to discover the underlying metaphorical logic of the text, and to recreate its effect for the reader of the translation, as far as possible. Otherwise, technical accuracy runs the risk of remaining obscure and, what is sometimes worse, inelegant; the academic tendency to use precise terms of Latin origin all too often conflicts with the best standards of prose style.

In addition, the vocabulary range of classical Arabic is far removed from that of modern English. There are, for example, several different words common in mystical texts, derived from the Arabic root relating to the number one, which are hard to distinguish in translation. The word *wahda* means numerical oneness, *tawhid* means affirming the unity of God, *wahdaniyya* implies a metaphysical unity, and *ittihad* refers to attaining union with God. The English words "unity" and "oneness" do not ordinarily carry such shades of precision, so it is necessary to use context and sometimes paraphrase to get the right meaning across. Another term that has proved difficult is *baqaʾ*, which is often translated by abstract terms like "abiding" or "subsistence." Frequently it is paired with *fanaʾ* or annihilation, and it stands for the apprehension of the divine eternal presence when the finite and created vanish away. The term has no clear subject, however; who is it that remains after the ego has been annihilated? Here too I have resorted to paraphrases about God becoming present, rather than settling upon a single English word.

A more formidable challenge for translation is presented by *iltibas,* a technical term that has a unique significance for Ruzbihan, and which is centrally related to the key symbol of veiling and unveiling. Literally meaning "clothing" or "cloaking," it invokes a semantic field associated with symbolic power, derived from the ritual garments presented by caliphs and princes to their followers at court, as well as with the robes of initiation given to disciples by Sufi masters. In a society which lacks this kind of ritual, it is hard to convey such associations; "investiture" is a term used in the middle ages for ritual clothing with the garments of ecclesiastical office, but this is unfortunately too archaic. *Iltibas* can also have an abstract meaning of "shrouding," with the connotation of concealing or hiding beneath an appearance. For Ruzbihan, this term can also signify a kind of veil of light in which God arrays himself in order to become visible, or in which he arrays a human who is thus endowed with the qualities of God. It therefore simultaneously conveys associations of symbolic power, concealment, and the luminous display of divine qualities. I have translated it in several different ways according to context, always trying to preserve the metaphor of cloaking or arraying.

With these concerns in mind, since this book is aimed at a wider audience, in a number of cases I have revised for readability passages that appeared in more literal versions in *Ruzbihan Baqli: Mystical Experience and the Rhetoric of Sainthood in Persian Sufism*. Unlike the passages quoted in that book, this translation gives all formulas of blessing in full, usually in parentheses, for the sake of completeness. The Arabic text consistently attaches certain phrases to almost every mention of God, which are translated here either in adjectival form as "God most high" (alternatively "transcendent God") or as a parenthetical phrase: "God (glory be to him)." Ruzbihan alternates between referring to God *(allah)* and the Truth *(al-haqq)*, and that distinction is observed in the translation. The blessings on the Prophet Muhammad and others in the manuscripts are frequently only indicated by a scribal abbreviation, so these formulas have therefore not been as regularly inserted in the translation. I have left pronouns and adjectives referring to God in the lower case, while names of God are capitalized. Words in square brackets are additions to the text designed to bring out meanings or references that are presupposed but not explicit.

It remains for me to thank in particular the publisher of Parvardigar Press, my wife Judith Ernst, who encouraged me to complete this translation, and who has closely overseen all aspects of its preparation. Editor Maura High made many valuable suggestions about the style appropriate for translating a mystical text into English, and she saved me from a number of infelicitous expressions; if I have not always followed her advice, I have only myself to blame. Joyce Kachergis and Anne Theilgard of Kachergis Book Design did a superb job of book production. Dr. Javad Nurbakhsh, head of the Nimatullahi Sufi order, graciously contributed an eloquent appreciation of Ruzbihan for the epigraph to this book. Thanks also to other good friends who encouraged me with this project, particularly Lyn Ott and John Bussanich. The illustration on the front cover and title page is reproduced by the kind permission of the Bibliothèque Nationale, Paris. This book is dedicated with gratitude to the memory of the two great French scholars who first made Ruzbihan Baqli known in the West: Louis Massignon and Henry Corbin.

Chapel Hill, North Carolina
November, 1996

PART ONE

THE MEMOIR

The Opening (✽ 1–6)

✽ 1. Benediction and Praise of God's Transcendence

In the name of God, the merciful, the compassionate. Praise belongs to God, in whose existence no doubt can be conceived, nor opinion, whose essence and attributes do not change with changing times and eons. His eternity has no measurable beginning, nor is his being limited in its implications. His pre-eternities are sanctified beyond the intervals of time, and his post-eternities are sanctified beyond the moment and the instant. He is known by his essence and his attributes to those who witness him, although in his essence and his attributes his self-knowledge is beyond proofs and evidence. Substances and accidents vanish in the fields of his oneness, and spirits and intellects are annihilated in the courtyards of his imperial splendor. He is in his essence isolated from fanciful allusions; his attributes are sanctified beyond the comprehension of intellects and imaginations. He was by virtue of his divinity before every existing being, and he will be by virtue of his power after all limits are passed. Lofty aspirations do not plumb the fullness of his depth, and searching intelligence does not scale the heaven of his attributes. There is no penetration of the secrets of his majesty, nor is there any comprehension of the lights of his beauty. The sublimities of his greatness obliterate vision, and the assaults of his magnificence erase thought. The power of his everlastingness confounds temporal understanding, and the wrath of his unity overpowers the constraints of space. His are the sublime attributes, the most beautiful names, and the most radiant qualities. He knows by his knowledge, is powerful by his power, lives by his life, hears by his hearing, sees by his seeing, speaks by his speech, and wills by his will. He is pre-eternal and post-eternal; he is being, but not from time; he is, but not from nothingness. By his essence and his attributes he is a mirror that is single from every perspective. His oneness is not from joining or from separation. He gave existence to the world, but not from loneliness. Bodies do not compare with him, nor do mortals resemble him. He is exalted by the quality of his glory beyond likenesses and equals; he is made one by the brilliance of his being, beyond imaginations, conceptions, and oppositions. Description does not disclose him, nor does effort entail his service.

✿ 2. The Unfolding of Creation, and Blessings on the Prophet

He brought forth for [humans] devotion and mystical knowledge, and he called them by his lordliness to humility and faith. He made the throne and the footstool into the treasuries of his kingdom, and he put in place the plain of his authority and the field of play for angels and spirits. He created the fire for the sorrowful and the garden for the happy. He unrolled the heavens with the tent ropes of nearness; he beautified them with the burning lights of the celestial realm, making the stars into the direction for prayer and the place of meditation for the people of praise. He unrolled the earths for the devotees and the kingdoms; he fastened them with the hardness of stones and pegs. He adorned them with graceful trees, and he made fountains and rivers flow. He singled out the spiritual ones for holiness and purity, and he chose the prophets and the messengers for revelation and prophecy. He selected the saints for ecstasies and sainthood, and he brought the sincere ones longing, passion, and love. He ennobled the prophets and the messengers with witnessing and vision; he opened the eyes of the saints' inner consciousness with unveilings and clarities, placing them at differing levels, ascensions, and stations. God bless Muhammad, the diver in the seas of mystical knowledge, unveilings, rare wisdom, and graces, the leader of the messengers and prophets, the model of the pure ones and the saints; bless his pure offspring and his noble companions.

❀ 3. God's Self-Revelation to His Lovers

Now God (glory be to him who is transcendent) taught the messengers, the prophets, the angels, and the saints about himself by special signs, from the throne to the earth; he taught them the signs in the beginnings, and they loved him because of his blessings and favor. But he was unsatisfied with what he had given them, for it was the cause of their creaturely condition. So he displayed to them the lights of his presence, anointed their eyes with the balm of might, and showed them the sunbeams of the world of his angelic realm. Now they loved him with a special love, but this love is in reality love of the beginning of the end. Then he unveiled to them the sublimities of his beauty and his majesty, manifesting his essence and his attributes. They knew him and loved him with the great, true love that does not alter with the changing of time, nor with the onset of afflictions and challenges. They witnessed him with the witnessing of reality without a veil. Then he addressed them and spoke to them of rare knowledge and wisdom. He instructed them in the incantations of his names, and he taught them the subtleties of his qualities and characteristics. He made them inhale the perfumed breezes of the rose of near encounters and the herbs of proximities and unions. He was expansive to them with his generous, intimate conversations, unveiled his secrets, was intimate with them with his beauty, and made them lovers with his majesty. By these degrees, they bore what they could of the weight of ascetic practices and strivings. They became the brides of his presence and the men of his kingdom and his angelic realm. Some of them are disciples, and some are saints; some are the people of signs, and some are the people of speeches, counsels, and intimate conversations; some are the people of unveilings, and some are the people of witnessings and conceptions; some are the people of mystical knowledge and grace, and some are the people of divine knowledge and wisdom; some are the people of unity, singleness, and isolation, some are the people of distinction, and some are the people of union. If they reach [their goal] and cross the ocean of pre-eternities and eternities, they become raving drunkards. If they remain settled and stand firm in the surging of the disasters of the hidden, from unveilings and ecstasies, they become the sober ones. If they reach the position of standing firm after being ravished, God most high makes them the lamps of the age, the signs of mystical knowledge, the stages of reality, and the guideposts of the religious law—may God place us and you among the people of these states and stations.

✿ 4. A Friend Asks for Guidance

Once, a lover (one of the sincere ones who leave behind existing things and time, seeking through isolation mystical knowledge and oneness) asked me with a perfect love to tell him the secrets of the unveilings and witnessings that occur to me, of the brides of the angelic realm and the wonders of the lights of power that are unveiled to me, of the particularities of God's manifestation and descent in the station where one is clothed with divinity, of the pure unveiling of the sublimities of God's essence, in my ecstasies, my intoxication, and my sobriety, by day and by night, and of the unknown sciences that God most high opened to me from his presence; thus it would be for him the proclamation of his path and his intimate companion in his heart and spirit in the hidden world.

✸ 5. The Problem of Sainthood and Prophethood

I answered him regarding this, and I heard his request. I said, "This is difficult for me, because it is very hard to present these mystical stages when the people of ordinary knowledge do not comprehend them. They criticize us and censure this; they fall into the ocean of affliction. I fear that the people of Muhammad (God's blessings upon him) will fall into denial and opposition; they will be destroyed, for one who does not believe in the unveilings of the sincere ones does not believe in the miracles of the prophets and messengers (blessings and peace upon them). For the oceans of sainthood and prophethood interpenetrate each other." God most high has said, "He has loosed the two oceans so that they meet" [Qur'an 55:19]. Nowadays, in the display of the experiences of the Folk [the Sufis], there have been events of rare kinds of knowledge, and marvellous unveilings in various forms, since the Truth has displayed himself in the clothing of the Creator, just as he manifested himself to the prophets, as he said regarding the Speaker [Moses]: "He was called from the right side of the valley in the blessed spot, from the tree: 'O Moses! I am I, God, the Lord of creation'" [Qur'an 28:30]. And just as he related regarding the Lover [Muhammad], when he manifested his beauty from "the lotus tree of the farthest limit, near which is the garden of Abode, when the lotus tree was concealed by that which concealed it" [Qur'an 53:14–16]. And just as he [Muhammad] related concerning the unveiling of the divine raiment, when he said, "I saw my lord in the most beautiful form. Then God said, 'Ask, Muhammad.' So I said, 'God! I ask you for paradise, and the love of those who love you.' Then he said, 'Muhammad, what does the highest assembly [of an-

gels] debate?' [see Qur'an 38:69]. I said, 'Lord, you know best.'
Then he placed his hand on my shoulder, and I felt a cool tingling
in my breast, and I knew what was and what will be."

❀ 6. The Tale Begins

So I said, "My friend, I have delayed in responding to your de-
mand for these exemplary stations and these noble states. I was in
my youth, and the days of my intoxication, extravagance, and
effervescence. Unveilings of the angelic world and the manifestation of the wonders of power took place in my heart, spirit, conscience, and intellect. I swam in the primordial and ultimate
oceans, in eternity and divine presence, and I discovered the unveiling of God's attributes and essence, which massive stones and
lofty mountains cannot bear. If I wrote down all that happened to
me from the beginning of my life to now, it would make a heavy
load of books and pages."

The Early Years (❀ 7–13)

❀ 7. Explaining Past Experience

I was fifteen years old when the beginnings of these secrets occurred in my heart. I am now fifty-five; how shall I explain to you the secrets of my unveilings, and my subtle witnessings, things that have escaped you? But I shall explain some things that were unveiled to me in days past, and I shall mention to you what happened to me after that, if God most high wills.

❀ 8. The Earliest Presentiments

Understand (and may God bless your understanding!) that I was born among ignorant drunkards who had gone astray, and was raised by common people of the market, "as though they were asses taking fright, fleeing from a lion" [Qurʾan 74:50–51], up to the age of three. The question occurred to my heart, "Where is your God, the God of creation?" We had a mosque at the gate of my house. I saw some children and asked them, "Do you know your God?" They said, "It is said that he has no hands or feet." For they had heard from their fathers and mothers that God most high transcends limbs and members. But when I asked that question, I was filled with endless joy. Something happened to me that is like what happens with the illuminations that occur while remembering God's names [*dhikr*], and the visitations of meditation, but I did not know the reality of what happened.

❀ 9. The Awakening of Love

I reached the age of seven, and in my heart there occurred a love of remembering and obeying him, and I sought my conscience and I learned what it was. Then passionate love occurred in my heart; my heart melted in passionate love. I was mad with love in that time, and my heart was at that time a diver in the ocean of pre-eternal remembrance and in the scent of the perfumes of sanctity. Then visitations of ecstasies appeared within me without causing any distress, a delicate emotion agitated my heart, and my eyes filled with tears. I knew not what it could be but the remembrance of the names of God most high. And at that time I was seeing all of existence as though it was beautiful faces, and during this period I grew fond of seclusions, prayers, devotions, and pilgrimage to the great shaykhs.

❀ 10. Entering the Mystical Path

When I reached fifteen years, it was as though I was addressed from the hidden world, and it was said to me, "You are a prophet." I said in my conscience, "I have heard from my parents that 'There is no prophet after Muhammad,' so how can I be a prophet, when I eat and drink, answer the call of nature, and have private parts?" For I thought that the prophets do not have these defects. Time passed, and I was lost in passionate love. I arose from my shop for afternoon prayers, and I went out into the desert seeking water for ablutions. I heard a beautiful voice, and my conscience and my heart were agitated. I said, "You who speak! Stay with me!" I climbed upon a hill near me, and I saw a beautiful person in the dress of the shaykhs, but I was unable to speak. He said something concerning the divine oneness, but I knew nothing about it. A ravishing and a bewilderment befell me.

❀ 11. Flight to the Desert

I was afraid, and people were walking around. I was out in a ruin, and remained there till night fell. Then I left and returned to my shop, and remained there until dawn in ecstasy, distress, sighs, and tears. I was astonished and bewildered. On my tongue without volition came the words, "Your forgiveness! Your forgiveness!" [Qur'an 2:285]. My tongue was stilled, and it was as though I was sitting for days together. I sat there another hour. Then ecstasy overwhelmed me, and I threw into the road the money box and whatever was in the shop for time of scarcity. I tore my clothes and headed to the desert. I remained in that state a year and a half, ravished and astonished, weeping and ecstatic. Great ecstasies and hidden visitations happened every day. In those ecstasies I saw the heavens, the earth, mountains, deserts, and trees as though they were all light. Then I settled down from that distress.

❀ 12. The First Unveiling

I had recovered from that veiling [of my early life], and I longed for the service of the Sufis. So I shaved my head, though I had fine and beautiful hair. I entered among the Sufis, and worked in their service, and undertook strivings and exercises. I studied the Qur'an and memorized it. Most of my time was spent among the Sufis, in ecstasy and spiritual states. But nothing in the way of hidden unveilings happened to me until one day I was on the roof of the lodge, meditating on the hidden world. And I saw the Prophet (God's blessings upon him), with Abu Bakr, ʿUmar, ʿUthman, and ʿAli (may God be pleased with them) passing in front of me, and this was my first unveiling.

✹ 13. Finding a Master

But I did not have a master at that time, and I returned to my home [Pasa] seeking a master and guide who was one of the saved. Then God most high guided me to Shaykh Jamal al-Din Abi al-Wafaʾ ibn Khalil al-Fasaʾi (may God have mercy on him), and he too was a beginner. And God most high in his company opened to me the doors of the angelic realm and uninterrupted unveilings, and in his company spiritual states overflowed with hidden sciences and religious mysteries, until innumerable ecstasies and unveilings took place.

❀ 14. The Friend of God

Among all that I have recalled, I saw God (glory be
to him) on the roof of my house, with the qualities of
might, majesty, and eternity. I saw as it were the
world entire, a resplendent light, manifold and great.
And he called me from the midst of the light, in the
Persian tongue, seventy times: "Ruzbihan, I have
chosen you for sainthood [*wilaya*] and selected you
for love. You are my friend [*wali*] and lover. Fear not
nor sorrow, for I am your God, and I keep watch
over you in your every aim." I was kneeling, and I
kneeled repeatedly. Then the oceans of ecstasies
seized me, I was overwhelmed by sobbing and increasing cries; I received much blessing from that.

❀ 15. The Castle of Sanctity

What I remember from the days of my youth is
that there was revealed to me in the hidden deserts
above the seven heavens a great ocean, and I saw in
the middle of the ocean a great island. And I saw in
the middle of the island a great castle of unlimited
height, and from the base of the castle as far upward
as I could see were innumerable windows. God most
high manifested to me from every window. I said,
"God! What is this ocean?" He said, "The ocean of
sanctity." And I said, "What is this island?" He said,
"The island of sanctity." And I said, "What is this

castle?" He said, "The castle of sanctity." God most high transcends the accident of space.

❀ 16. The Apple of Khidr

At that time I was ignorant of the sciences of realities. And I saw [the immortal prophet] Khidr (peace be upon him), and he gave me an apple, and I ate a piece of it. Then he said, "Eat all of it, for that is how much of it I ate." And I saw as it were an ocean from the throne to the earth, and I saw nothing but this; it was like the radiance of the sun. My mouth opened involuntarily, and all of it entered into my mouth. I drank until not a single drop of it remained.

❀ 17. Swimming the Ocean like ʿAli

One day I also saw as though I were on the mountain of the east, and I saw a group of angels. There was an ocean that seemed to go from east to west, and I saw nothing beyond this. And they said to me, "Enter this sea, and swim in it to the west." So I entered the sea, and swam in it. And when I reached the place of the sun at evening time, I saw the mountains of the east and west like little hills. I saw a group of angels on the mountain of the west, and they were glowing with the light of the sun. They shouted and said, "Whoever you are, swim and do not be afraid." So when I reached the mountain they said, "No one has crossed this ocean except [the fourth caliph,] ʿAli ibn Abi Talib (God ennoble his countenance), and you after him."

❁ 18. Experience beyond Religious Knowledge

Then after that, the gates to the sciences of divine presence were opened to me, the realities, subtleties, and unknown sciences, in which the understanding of the religious scholars is astonished. Then certain of my prayers were answered, and miraculous graces occurred. My consciousness was grounded in realities, while the ascension of ascensions appeared to me. I attained stations, states, unveilings, mystical knowledge, divine oneness, and innumerable unveilings of the hidden in hearts of wonder.

❁ 19. The Oil of the Little Bear

I also saw all of humanity in a house holding a feast, with many lamps among them, though it was day. I could not reach them, so I went on the roof of the house, and I saw two handsome shaykhs in Sufi dress, who looked like me. I saw a kettle suspended in the air, and the firewood of the two shaykhs burned with a subtle burning, without smoke. I saw a tablecloth hanging from their tent. I greeted them, and they faced me and smiled; they were good-looking shaykhs. One of them took his tablecloth and opened it up, and on the tablecloth was a lovely bowl and some loaves of pure white bread. He broke some of the loaves in the bowl and upended over the bowl the contents of the kettle, which was like a pale oil, weightless, but with a subtle spiritual substance. He gestured to me, indicating that I should eat, so I ate some. They ate a little with me, until I ate it all. One of them said, "Don't you know what was in the kettle?" I said, "I do not know." He said, "This is the oil of the Little Bear; we got it for you." When I stood up, I thought about it. It was some time later that I realized that this was an allusion to the seven poles [qutbs] in the angelic realm, and that God most high had chosen me for the pure essence of their stations, which is the rank of the seven who are on the face of the earth. Then I turned toward the constellation of the Little Bear, and I saw that the stars were seven windows, from all of which God most high manifested to me. I said, "My God! What is this?" God, who transcends every imagination, said, "These are the seven windows of the throne."

✸ 20. The Windows of Heaven

Time passed, and I was thinking about them every night, from love and longing for them. One night I saw that they were opened. I saw the Truth, who is glorious and transcendent, appearing from them, saying, "I appeared to you from these windows; these windows are seventy thousand gates to the great world of the angelic. I manifested myself to you from all of them—understand that." I passed with my conscience through the regions of the created, and my spirit ascended to the heavens. I saw in every heaven the angels of God most high, but I passed them by until I reached the presence. I saw that his creations, the angels, were greater than his creatures on earth; they were performing prayer, witnessing the nearness of the Truth, with voices thundering his praise. Then I rose up to the world of shining light to ask about it, and I was told that this world is called the throne. I trembled through an atmosphere without dimension, until I reached the doors of eternity. There I saw deserts and oceans; I was being annihilated, I was bewildered, vanishing, astonished, not knowing from where the Truth appeared, for there was no where or whence.

✸ 21. The Chosen One of God

He manifested himself to me in the form of eternity, from the dawns of the beginning, saying to me, "I traveled to you from the hidden of the hidden, and the hidden of the hidden; between you and me was a journey of seven hundred thousand years." He addressed me lovingly and was kind to me and compassionate to me. He said, "I have chosen you in your time for this station over all creatures." He unveiled the holy virtues and the chosen attributes of pre-eternity. I saw a beauty in majesty, and a majesty in beauty, which I will never be able to describe. One of the things he bequeathed to me was that perfect love and special knowledge. He placed me before him, and he appeared each moment with a thousand kinds of glory, brilliance, light, and radiance.

✾ 22. The King of Persia

In the days of my youth, I used to keep vigil in the middle of the night. I prayed one night, and the Truth (glory be to him) passed me by "in the most beautiful form." He laughed in my face and threw me a bag of musk. I said, "Give me more than that." He said, "Both of them are kings, but you are the king of Persia."

✾ 23. God the Giver

I was wakeful one night at midnight; I was between sleep and waking, but not alert. But in my changeableness I said, "Giver!" And the Truth (great is his majesty) appeared with the quality of majesty and beauty, manifest and adorned with jewels of light. He scattered on me a great abundance, a largess that was scattered from his eternal countenance. He said, "Since you called out, 'Giver,' take this from the Giver, for I am the generous Giver."

✾ 24. Paradise on the Night of Power

Not a year passed that God most high did not unveil to me the Night of Power, and show me all of the angels in the form of man, laughing, greeting one another. Gabriel was among them, and he is the most beautiful of the angels. The angels have hair like women, and their faces are like red roses. Some have veils of light on their heads, some wear jeweled hats on their heads, and some wear garments of pearls. Often I saw them in the form of Turks. I saw Ridwan and the garden, and I entered it. I saw the houris and heavenly youths just as God most high described them [in the Qur'an]. I entered the castles and drank from streams; I ate the fruits of the garden, and I ate melons in the garden. Often I saw the throne and the footstool, and I saw God most high clothed with divinity, as if he were a master wearing a cloak; I melted from his majesty and grandeur.

✢ 25. The Gown of Might

I saw one night something encompassing the heavens, and it was a red light shining like pearl. I said, "What is this?" I was told, "This is the gown of might." The Truth, who is transcendent, received me between the throne and the footstool, with legs bared [from tying the gown in readiness], with satisfaction and joy.

✢ 26. In the Divine Presence
with the Prophets

One night I entered the presence, and I saw the Truth in his greatness and magnificence. I saw in the [divine] presence Adam, Noah, Abraham, Moses, Jesus, and our Prophet Muhammad (blessings upon him). I reached the place of utter nearness, and they descended upon me. He graced me with things such that, if all of creation heard a word of it, they would have died of grief in the veils of the hidden and the coverings of the kingdom and the angelic realm; at last I departed from the world and creation.

✣ 27. The Throne Beneath the Earth

I saw myself beneath the earth, in an atmosphere of light. The Truth appeared to me there (great is his majesty). I said, "My God! I sought you above every above, but now I see you in this world below the earth." And he did something that I did not understand. I saw the throne beneath the earth, in his hands, like a mustard seed in the desert. He said, "I transform the world and what is in it, and nothing temporal harms me. I transcend the imaginations of charlatans and the allusions of analogists." God is beyond all space and likenesses. These unveilings are according to the principles of the states of the knowers of God and the value of their attainments.

✣ 28. The Ditches of Blood

I saw one night the presence of the Truth, who is transcendent, and he took me and slaughtered me. Much blood poured from my neck, and all the ditches filled up with my blood. My blood was like the shining of the rising sun, greater than the regions of the heavens and the earth. Crowds of angels took my blood and anointed their faces with it.

✣ 29. Physical Initiations from the Prophet

I saw our Prophet Muhammad (peace be upon him) in various clothes more than a thousand times. I ate dates from his hand; he put a date in my mouth and said, "Eat it with the permission of God and the blessing of God." He gave me his tongue one night, and I mouthed it. One night he put a turban on my head.

❀ 30. The Ocean of Wine

I saw one night a great ocean in the hidden world, and the sea was of red wine. I saw the Prophet sitting cross-legged in the midst of the deep ocean, drunk, wearing gold-embroidered clothes and a gold-embroidered turban on his head. In his hand was a cup of wine from that ocean. When he saw me, he emptied it out and scooped up a cup of wine from that ocean, and then he emptied it out again, repeatedly. Then he plunged his hand into the ocean with the cup, filled it with the pure liquid, and gave it to me to drink. After that something was revealed to me, and I realized that he is superior to all the rest of creation, since they die thirsty and he is drunk in the midst of the ocean of majesty.

❀ 31. "The Praiseworthy Station"

It often came to my mind in the past: What is the meaning of "the praiseworthy station" [Qurʾan 17:79]? And one night in the divine presence I saw a mighty ocean without shore, and I saw all the prophets unclothed in the ocean, and also all the angels and the saints. I saw a thick veil hanging down [from heaven] to the ocean. I saw Adam in the ocean, and the ocean was up to his chest. Anyone closer to God most high would have been closer to him than that veil. Adam and "the resolute prophets" [Qurʾan 46:35] were in front of the veil. I went closer to the veil. Then I wanted to learn what was beyond the veil, so I went to the edge of the veil. When I reached it, I saw coming from beyond the veil a great light, and I saw a person like the moon from head to foot. His face was like the face of the moon, and he was greater than the heavens in their entirety. That person had seized the whole divine presence; there was not a point as big as the head of a pin that was not filled with it. There was upon his face a continuous light from the divine presence, without interruption. I wanted to go in beyond the veil but was unable to do so. So I said to myself, "What place is this? And who is this person?" And a call came in my consciousness "This is the praiseworthy station, and that is Muhammad (peace be upon him), and that which you see on his face is the light of manifestation. If you had been able to enter, you would have seen God (glory be to him who is transcendent) without a veil." And it was said to me, "This station is exclusively Muhammad's, and no one else has access to this station."

✿ 32. Consuming the Scriptures

I saw in the hidden world a world illuminated from a shining light. I saw the Truth (glory be to him) in the clothing of majesty, beauty, and glory; he poured me a drink from the ocean of affection, and he honored me with the station of intimacy. He showed me the world of holiness, and when I passed through the atmosphere of eternity, I stopped at the door of power. I saw all the prophets present there; I saw Moses with the Torah in his hand, Jesus with the Gospel in his hand, David with the Psalms in his hand, and Muhammad with the Qurʾan in his hand. Moses gave me the Torah to eat, Jesus gave me the Gospel to eat, David gave me the Psalms to eat, and Muhammad gave me the Qurʾan to eat. Adam gave me the most beautiful names [of God] and the Greatest Name to drink. I learned what I learned of the elect lordly sciences for which God singles out his prophets and saints.

✿ 33. The Turkish Musician

I saw myself as though I were in Turkistan, and the Truth appeared to me from the east in the garb of the Turks, playing on one of their stringed instruments. He said, "I appeared to you from the wombs of pre-eternity." He showed me the beautiful attributes, and he came to me and was kind to me. Then he hid from me, so that I complained to him about that. Then the Truth appeared to me in a form more beautiful than I had ever seen.

✦ 34. The Self-Blaming Master in the Desert

In my youth I had a master, a knower of God who was intoxicated all the time; he was a self-blaming [*malamati*] master whose nature was unknown. One night I saw a desert in the deserts of the hidden world, and I saw the Truth (who is transcendent) in the form of that master sitting at the edge of the desert. I went down to him, and he indicated to me another desert. I went to that desert, and I saw a master like him, and that master was the Truth. He indicated to me another desert, so that seventy thousand deserts were unveiled to me, and at the edge of each desert I saw the like of what I had seen in the first. I said to myself, "God most high is one, single, solitary, and separate; he transcends scarcity, multitude, number, opposites, and likenesses." And it was said to me, "These are the manifestations of the primordial attributes, which are unlimited." At that moment the realities of oneness from the ocean of magnificence overwhelmed me, because the Truth (who is transcendent) manifests himself in the form of awe.

✦ 35. Moses Disappearing on Mount Sinai

I also saw the Truth (glory be to him) descend from Mount Sinai in the dress of a great shaykh, and the mountain melted under the assaults of his powerful wrath. He disappeared, then he appeared, then he disappeared, then he appeared, repeatedly. Then he said, "Thus I have done to Moses."

✤ 36. The Spinning of the Shepherd

I saw the Truth (glory be to him who is transcendent) in the dress of a shepherd with a spindle in his hand, spinning the throne, wearing clothes of rough white wool [*suf*]. I remembered in my heart that this is a kind of similitude, and God most high transcends the imagination. How can I say this is the God of earth and heaven? But I saw the throne being wound around the spindle like fleece. I was astonished and drowned in the ocean of magnificence. Then he hid from me.

✤ 37. Angels with Tresses

I repeatedly saw him with the quality of majesty and beauty. With him were angels like beautiful women, with tresses so long that if one of them grew any longer, it would touch the earth. I said, "My God! How will you seize my spirit?" He said, "I will come to you from the wombs of pre-eternity. I will seize your spirit with my hand, and I will take it to the station of nearness. I will give you to drink the wine of nearness, and I will show you my beauty and my majesty, for ever, just as you wish, without a veil." I saw Gabriel, Michael, Israfil, and Azraʾil (peace be upon them) in clothes of light, with a beauty I am unable to describe. I saw Munkir and Nakir [the two angels who interrogate the souls of the dead], like two handsome, beautiful youths, playing the lute on my tombstone, saying, "We are lovers for you; we shall enter your tomb in this form." Fear fell away from me.

✤ 38. The Death of a Friend

One of my companions died. I saw a desert beyond the seven heavens, made of red clay, filled with the dead, lying on their shrouds. I said, "What is this desert?" They said, "This is the place of the martyrs of God and his pure ones." I saw a funeral bier borne on the shoulders of the angels; they brought it and put it down. I saw the Truth (glory be to him who is transcendent) praying over it—God most high was praying over all of them. I asked, "Who is this person?" They said, "Your companion." I wept bitterly, for he was a youth from among us. Then I saw him on a wall of the orchards in paradise, and I said, "Master! What are you doing?" He spread his hands and built a wall from blue sapphires, saying, "I am preparing your house and your orchards in paradise."

❁ 39. The World of Roses

Often I saw the Truth (who is transcendent) between the rose tent, the rose veil, and the world of red and white roses. He showered many roses, pearls, and rubies on me, and I drank much from the wine of the springs he has in the abode of sanctity. Mysteries of expansiveness took place between me and him. If anyone saw me at that time, he would accuse me of heresy, not knowing that this is the expansiveness of the Truth (who is transcendent) toward his saints, and the appearance of the graces of his righteousness. Otherwise, what would become of time in the crashing waves of the oceans of pre-eternity, and the storm of greatness, when even Mount Qaf flees from the display of these assaults of beauty? God transcends the allusion of the analogist; may God most high nourish this creation with a perfect intellect.

❁ 40. On the Carpet of Oneness
without a Veil

What we have shown and alluded to is a kind of knowledge that comes from the sciences of passion and love. The Truth appeared here in beauty and majesty, and he bequeathed to them some of that love, passion, and knowledge. This is because there are seas of unknowing in the reality of the divine oneness, from which all the prophets, messengers, angels, and saints flee. In the station of divine oneness is the burning of greatness, which consumes thoughts, understandings, and comprehensions. There is no god but God—glory be to him beyond what intellects ascribe to him. Now one night it happened that I was sitting on the bench in my house, in the middle of the latter part of the night, in a state of meditation. My thoughts observed the throng of unveilings, and the appearance of the pennants of the world of the angelic. I was gazing with the eyes of conscience at the beings illuminated by the attributes. I gazed around the hidden heavens until an hour passed for me. The Truth appeared to me in majesty and beauty from the window of pre-eternity. I saw the joy of satisfaction in the face of eternity. He made me see the majesty and beauty, the attractiveness and glory and expansiveness that he sees. I entered into ecstasy and cried out repeatedly, annihilated in his majesty. But between us lay the deserts of the hidden, and the veils of jealousy, throughout the atmosphere of ʿIlliyyin [the highest heaven]. I wanted to spend time with him, because of my nearness to him. I saw him, and he had just left one of the rooms of my house, "in the most beautiful of forms." He made my heart jealous, and he annihilated my conscience. I melted from the sweetness of witnessing him, and from his kindness. Then he became visible to me in another form, and he drew near to his weak slave, to the utmost nearness. Then he hid, and he manifested himself from the essence of divinity in the world of eternity, as divine oneness and singleness. I was astonished at his dignity and at the ecstasy he had ordained for me, and the various unveilings. Then he appeared to me from beyond the throne, in the clothing of glory and beauty. I saw on the throne a garment woven of light. He called me from beyond it, but he was not veiled by it. I saw him unveiled, and he said, "Ruzbihan! Do not shed tears at the shifting flow of the shapes of the actions, and do not doubt what you have seen; 'I am I' [Qurʾan 28:30), your lord, the one, the single. You do not deserve that I should distress you in the oceans of unknowing. I am yours throughout my creation, so do not worry over anything. I shall convey you to the station of 'the vision of vision,' and I shall seat you on the carpet of my nearness forever, without a veil."

Confirmation by the Saints of Persia (❀ 41–45)

❀ 41. The Pass of the Jinn

I happened to arrive at the town of Khir, and it was difficult for me and my companions to depart from it, due to a lack of animals we could use as mounts. And I saw the shaykh Abu [Muslim] al-Faris as though he came out of his tomb, and he said, "Do not worry! Stay there, for I am with you." And he took the staffs of my companions and went. While we were there, someone came with a guide, asses, and supplies. We traveled half the night on that road. There were many mountains in that place, and a mountain was in our path, which crossed a pass called the Pass of the Jinn. We lost the path repeatedly, and we traveled in indescribable fear and suffering. We went on like that until dawn, and when we found ourselves near the town of Pasa, we were overjoyed. When we reached the city and stopped at the lodge of Shaykh Abu Muhammad al-Jawzak, we spent the night there and slept. I arose for devotions at dawn, and I performed ablutions and prayed two cycles of prayer, and stood for the third. And I thanked God most high, for he had saved us from those mountains and their passes.

❀ 42. God's Mercy on the Mountain

The Truth addressed me with the special address reserved for unveiling and witnessing. He said, "Ruzbihan! Why do you worry? I have descended from the mountain and ascended it for you and for [your] protection nine times." When I heard the speech of the Truth (who is transcendent) in this form, every atom of my soul was filled with sparks of the fire of greatness. If I had heard on the mountain what I had heard at the residence, I would have flown from the mountain top. I was annihilated. He made me comprehend the grace of my lord and his eternal mercy, for he is compassionate to his friends and merciful to his lovers.

✻ 43. At the Tomb of Abu Muslim

When I left Abun, I went to the tomb of Shaykh Abu Muslim [al-Faris] to apologize for my bad manners. As I approached his grave, I did not find sensitivity in my heart, and I was worried about that. When I saw the tomb of the shaykh, I began to feel ecstasy, my heart became sensitive, and I started to weep profusely. Then I turned, and I saw the masters of Abu Yazid among the grandsons of the master. I departed raving, and took to the road. A voice called to me in my heart, saying "A near punishment should seize you" [Qur'an 7:73]. The voice filled me with fear, and I was afraid that calamity would befall me. So we traveled that day until we reached al-Sanjat and stayed in the lodge of Hanyan, spending the night there. That message descended on my heart repeatedly, until I performed sunset prayers. My heart was agitated and my conscience simmered.

✻ 44. The Camel of God

At that moment I saw the lights of the hidden and the traces of the Truth. I saw the masters of India saluting me, and the masters of Turkistan and the masters of Khurasan and Persia blessing me. And I saw Shaykh Abu Muslim Faris ibn al-Muzaffar, Shaykh Abu

Bakr al-Khurasani, Shaykh Abu al-Qasim al-Darijirdi, and Shaykh Abu ʿAbd Allah ibn Khafif (God have mercy on them) riding together. Shaykh Abu Muslim gleamed with light, and he spoke to the people of the day, indicating me [with the words of the prophet Salih to the ancient Arabian people of Thamud]: "This is the camel of God, a sign for you; let her feed on God's earth, and touch her not with evil, lest a near punishment should seize you" [Qurʾan 7:73]. And I realized that the first message [in ✡43] was connected to this message, and I was extremely glad about that message, for it likened me to the camel of God, which is the greatest of signs.

✡ 45. Seeking the Vision of the Essence

The Truth addressed me after that special address [✡42] by which he chose for himself his friends and his chosen ones, saying, "I shall make you enter into the orchards of holiness, and I shall show you my witnessing; do not fear, for you are one of my chosen few." I saw the Truth in the form of majesty and beauty, magnificence and greatness; I saw intimations of the cloak of divinity, and I said, "My God, my friend, and my lord, how long will you make me see the chosen vision within the limits of the cloak of divinity? Show me pure eternity and divine presence!" And he said, "Moses and Jesus perish in this station." And the Truth (who is transcendent) revealed himself in an atom of the light of his pre-eternal essence (he is mighty and supreme), and my spirit nearly vanished. Despite that, I feared death, lest the end of my life should take place in just such a feebleness as was my state at that hour. And I saw our prophet Muhammad, all the prophets (peace be upon them), all his companions (may God be pleased with them), and all the masters (God have mercy on them) asking God most high to nourish me with the station of greatness.

Further Early Visions (✵ 46–49)

✵ 46. Lights during Sickness

Once I was sick, troubled by fever in the night. I awakened after half the night, and was lying down, as is customary with the sick, with my family. And I saw myself in one of the rooms of the angelic world. Lights were unveiled to me, and the Truth (who is transcendent) appeared to me, and my soul and form were nearly overthrown. God most high made his peace descend upon me, but the ecstatic dawns and sweet secrets did not cease. No one of my family nor anyone around me knew of that state.

✵ 47. The Light of the Countenance

And he, the Truth (who is transcendent), was with me another time. I saw that he glowed with a light, whiter than pearls or snow. Then the sound of stringed instruments emerged from the nearness of the Truth. I realized that this was healing me. The unveiling became complete, and the beautiful attributes appeared to me. The Truth (who is transcendent) honored me, no distance remained between us. I saw from the face of God most high a beauty and majesty and glory, from seeing which the inhabitants of heaven and earth would have all died from pleasure. Then I saw the regions of heaven and earth filled with him. And I was with him, until he made me present in the station of nearness of nearness, above everything, and he manifested upon me seventy thousand majesties, beauties, and perfections. He spoke to me with a voice that would have made Mount Qaf melt with pleasure, and all of that talk was talk of nearness and fondness. When he made me sit before him, and treated me with great kindness, he gave me to drink wines of his presence, wines that I am unable to describe. There appeared from the Truth (who is transcendent) sounds that cannot be expressed.

✿ 48. The Anointing of the Prophets

And when I became quiet, I thought, "Where is Muhammad (peace be upon him), and where are the prophets and messengers?" God (great is his majesty) spoke to me: "They have been annihilated in the lights of eternity." I saw the prophets departing like great drunkards from the lights of eternity, and all of them went in front of God most high. The first one to arrive was our prophet, [Muhammad], then Adam, then Noah, then Abraham, then Moses, then Jesus, then all the rest of the prophets. The Prophet [Muhammad] stopped, being the closest of creatures to God most high, and they formed a circle, and in the midst of the circle were [his four successors, the caliphs] Abu Bakr, ʿUmar, ʿUthman, and ʿAli (may God be pleased with them). God most high anointed the head of Muhammad, and then he anointed the heads of the prophets.

✿ 49. The Representative of God

And the armies of angels were seen emerging from the wombs of the hidden. Their leaders Gabriel, Michael, and Israfil are like Turks, and they have tresses like those of women. Then God most high anointed me with a largess of roses and pearls, as he did the prophets, the angels, and the four caliphs [✹48]. The Prophet spoke to me, kissed my face, and likewise Adam, Noah, Abraham, Moses, Jesus, and all the prophets, and likewise the four caliphs. Then God most high praised and prayed for Muhammad and his other prophets. Then he said, "I have chosen my servant Ruzbihan for pre-eternal happiness, sainthood, and miracles, and I have placed in him the receptacles of my knowledge and my secret; the conditions of separation will not trouble him after that. I have preserved him from disobeying me after that, and I have made him one of the people of stability and rectitude. He is my representative [*khalifa*] in this world and all worlds. I love whosoever loves him, and I hate whosoever hates him. None disobeys my judgments, and none rejects my order, for I am 'one who acts when he wishes'" [Qur'an 11:107].

Visions of Mecca (❁ 50–53)

❁ 50. A Dream of the Kaʿba of Light

I saw what a dreamer sees, as though I were in the sacred enclosure of God most high [in Mecca], and a light unlike the lights of the world was in the center of the mosque. I saw the Kaʿba in the midst of that light, with garments of special light upon it. I never saw the like of it. The brilliance of that light was like the brilliance of the throne. I wondered at the beauty of the house, and the radiance of the mosque. Then I awoke and stood for ablutions, and I entered the bath.

❁ 51. A Vision of Mecca in the Bath

I recalled what I saw in the dream, and I rejoiced in it intensely. I was thinking about the degree of the dream, and what things it could bring forth. It was as though I saw while awake many of the Prophet's companions in the sacred mosque, as though they were separating and joining together. I saw among them the Messenger of God (peace be upon him), as though he were a perfumed sphere of white light. He was taller than his companions, and he wore a garment of wool, with a hat on his head. He had the most beautiful kind of tresses, and his face was like the laughing sun. His aspects were more beautiful than crimson light. He summoned me as he stood behind the [well of] Zamzam, as though he were calling me from far away. He said, "You are the best of my people." I became proud because of what he said, and I wept intensely. After that my state quietened. My carnal self refused to believe me in these unveilings, because I saw them while I was still in the bath. Then I sought forgiveness in my conscience from God from the speech of my carnal self. God most high increased me in certainty, until my heart became strengthened in that which was revealed to me. So my carnal soul fled, as this is customary with this sign.

❀ 52. Ecstasies in the Kaʿba

I stood up after that to shout, and ecstasy overcame me. I saw as though I were in the sacred mosque, and I saw the Prophet, and it was as though he was in a state of ecstasy. He was turning around near the Black Stone, to the left of the Kaʿba, and Gabriel was standing by the pillar near the gate of al-Safaʾ. Michael was also standing near Gabriel, and Seraphiel was near them both, and a group of angels was standing on the floor of the mosque. I approached the Prophet in a state of astonishment. The Prophet turned toward me and called me by my name. Gabriel called out to me, saying, "Ruzbihan!" He was in ecstasy, and he called out to me again. Michael called out to me, and he also called me by my name. Seraphiel called me by name, and called out to me, saying, "Ruzbihan!" Gabriel was entering ecstasy, Seraphiel was entering ecstasy, and Michael was entering ecstasy. Every one of them left their places to be near the Prophet. I saw the Kaʿba as though it was leaving its place to be near them, and it danced with them. God most high manifested himself to them, and I among them was going into ecstasy and then settling down.

✸ 53. Paradise within the Mosque of Mecca

After that I was veiled for an hour, and I settled down from my ecstasy and the state in which I had been until dawn approached. Then ecstasy seized me, and a man was unveiled to me in the center of the sacred mosque, as though he were moving sand from the center of the mosque to one side, until a door appeared beneath the sand. That door was opened; he entered the door, and I entered after him. I saw one other man standing behind the door. The first man was Ishmael [son of Abraham and builder of the Kaʿba], and the other was Ridwan [guardian angel of Paradise]. When I entered the door, I saw the garden of paradise and everything in it, its trees, streams, and lights innumerable. In it I saw Muhammad, Adam, and all the prophets, saints, martyrs, and angels. I saw there a great crowd of the believers. I saw a world such that, if the heavens and earth were thrown into it, no one would find them, because of its greatness and extent. In that world I saw nothing I had seen in this world except light upon light, brilliance upon brilliance, glory upon glory, and kingdom upon kingdom.

To the Divine Court (❀ 54–56)

❀ 54. Riding with the Prophets

I saw our Prophet, all the prophets and messengers, and all the saints, riding on camels, and I was riding to the right of the Prophet. I saw upon them clothing of gold and pearl. It was as though they were in single file, speeding through an atmosphere like the pure red gold in the center of a flame. I saw Gabriel leading the people like a dove in the air. It was as though they were talking to one another, hurrying like soldiers at the time of muster. I recalled my companions and summoned them, and I saw them, according to the power of their states, both near and veering far, and I turned aside. There was one who rode behind me, wearing clothes as though they were of blue light; I never saw the like of it. He made his horse catch up to me, holding the horse's reins in his hand in the most beautiful way, and he talked with me.

❀ 55. Approaching the Divine Presence

We reached the presence of power that God had established. God unveiled to us our encounter with him, and he granted us peace. After that I saw none of God's creatures, so I remained alone and astonished, until the time that God most high had wished came to pass. God most high unveiled to me the veils of greatness, and I saw beyond the veils a majesty, a force, power and might, and oceans and lights, which are impossible to show to created beings. I was at the door of greatness like a bewildered beggar. He spoke to me from the pavilions of greatness, saying, "Beggar! How did you get here?" I felt expansive toward him and said, "My God, my friend, and my lord! With your favor, generosity, and munificence."

✣ 56. The Commitment to
Write of God's Graces

This is what I recall of what happened to me in days past. If I had remembered what I have forgotten, it would fill the pages of many books. Not a day or night has gone by me, except as God wished, from the time of my maturity until now, when I am fifty-five years old, without an unveiling of the hidden world. I saw then what I saw of great witnessings, eternal attributes, and prophetic ascensions time and again, and that is from the grace of God most high toward me. He gives to whom he wishes. "Grace is from the hand of God, and he gives to whom he wishes" [Qurʾan 3:73]. "He chooses for his mercy whom he wishes" [Qurʾan 2:105]. Praise be to God who ennobles by these stations his saints and his prophets without cause or reason, not because of their striving or discipline, not as the philosophers say—may God purify the earth of them! Now I will write, with God's aid, of the affairs of unveiling, the mysteries of witnessing, the marvels of the kingdom and the angelic realm, the gracious colloquies, and that which appears in ecstasies, God willing. He is my sufficiency in that, and "what an excellent one to trust" [Qurʾan 3:173].

PART TWO

THE DIARY

Ongoing Visions (❀ 57–210)

❀ 57. The Lion of Oneness

In one particular revelation I saw a tawny lion of mighty form, clothed with mighty power, walking on top of Mount Qaf. He ate up all the prophets, the messengers, and the saints, and their flesh remained in his mouth, and the blood dripped from it. I thought, "If I were there, would he eat me as he ate them?" And I found myself in his mouth, and he ate me. This is an allusion to the jealous wrath of the divine unity and its sovereignty, even over those who proclaim its unity. The Truth manifests the attributes of eternal greatness in the form of the lion. Its real significance is that the knower of God is a morsel for the wrath of unknowing in the station of annihilation.

❀ 58. "Seek Me in the Station of Love"

I saw in one of my unveilings a time when I sat in meditation, hunting the birds of the angelic realm, which fly in the world of might, with the nets of recollecting God's names [*dhikr*]. I was lifted up in the forms of actions and my will was to travel in eternity, but it was not possible for me to depart from the exterior of the actions. I saw the Truth (glory be to him who is transcendent) in "the most beautiful form." He dawned upon me suddenly from the hidden world, and I could not control myself, so that I sobbed and cried. Then this form approached, offered me hospitality, and set me ablaze with increased longing. It was as though he was scattering from his face white roses, and wearing pearl brocade. He hid from me, then he appeared to me, in a form more beautiful than the first. And I went until I was united with him. He said to me in my conscience, "Where are you going?" I said, "To eternity without end and without beginning." He said, "And what do you want?" I said, "I want my annihilation in the wrath of eternity, for I am not content with the vision of the cloak of divinity." He said, "This is a long journey. But I will come with you and be your companion on the path." So we went beyond the throne, and traveled on a journey to the hidden of the hidden. First he disappeared from me, then he appeared to me after an hour with the quality of power, and there I was annihilated. And he summoned me, saying, "Seek me in the station of love, for the world and everything in it are no match for the assaults of my glory." Then he appeared to me in a form more beautiful than any other, and the sweetness of that witnessing remained with me, but he did not give my desire to me. So I remained in the station of censuring and complaining about him until the time of dawn.

✪ 59. The Hand of God

I saw one evening a shimmering light, and I did not know what that light was. And God most high revealed his holy hand and showed me that what I saw of his light was from the glory of his hand. I saw nothing of him but his hand. And I loved it, for it transformed spirits, hearts, and intellects, and I saw nothing sweeter than this revelation. And I saw all existence like an atom between his fingers. I was prepared for the recitation of the saying of the Most High, "They do not measure the worth of God in truth, for the entire earth is in his grasp on the day of judgment, and the heavens are furled up in his right hand; glory be to him who transcends what they associate him with" [Qur'an 39:67]. God tran-

scends the thoughts that befall the hearts of the heedless and the ignorant, and the imaginations of the form of temporal shapes. In all
of his attributes he is beyond what opinions and thoughts ascribe
to him. His essence has no likeness, nor do his attributes have any
comparison. He is as he described himself in the saying of the Most
High, "There is no likeness unto him" [Qur'an 42:11].

✹ 60. The Face of Beauty

I sat in the middle of the night, past midnight, for meditation
and the journeying of consciences in the world of lights, seeking
the beauty of the overpowering king (glory be to the power of his
greatness). I suddenly saw in the middle of the road a transcendent
beauty I cannot describe. He was "in the most beautiful form," and
I fell in love with his beauty and his attributes. I longed to draw
near and be united with him, and he remained not far away. Then I
abased myself, and he appeared to me, then he hid, then he appeared, unveiled even by eternity. Where were the faces of those
brides of the angelic realm who have faces, and the houris of the
gardens? And where was the face of Adam and Joseph, in the presence of the beauty of the attributes, and the glories of his face? God
transcends all likeness and comparison.

✹ 61. The Vastness of the Heart

I saw him on the streets of the hidden with something in his
hand. I said, "My God, what is this?" He said, "Your heart." I said,
"Has my heart such a station that it lies in your hand?" He gazed at
my heart, and it was like something folded up, so he spread it out.
And my heart covered the space from the throne to the earth. I
said, "This is my heart?" He said, "This is your heart, and it is the
vastest thing in existence." He took it, as it was still in his hand, to
the angelic regions, and I went with him, until I reached the trea-

sury of the hidden of the hidden. I said, "Where are you taking it?" And he said, "To the world of eternity, so that I may look in it, and create the wonders of reality in it, and forever manifest myself in it with the attribute of divinity."

✿ 62. "Hearts Are between Two Fingers of the Merciful One"

And I said, "I want to see you with the quality you had in pre-eternity." He said, "There is no way for you to do that." And I abased myself and said, "I want that!" And the lights of greatness appeared, and I became vanishing, annihilated. Time does not abide after the whirlwind of greatness appears. Then my conscience was addressed, and it was said, "Do you know the meaning of the Prophet's words, 'Hearts are between two fingers of the Merciful One, who changes them as he wishes'?" That is what I saw between the fingers of the Transcendent One. That is the pillage of the hearts of his lovers, in which he changes them from the world to the fields of his majesty. And when he hid from me, I remembered two verses of eternity, and I was bequeathed this unveiling in my conscience with great happiness, at a time of sobriety.

✿ 63. Flight to the Royal Falconer

Then I was bequeathed happiness, visitations of ecstasy, and perfumes of the moment. The spiritual state and the happiness melted in his beauty and his nearness. It happened that between the evening prayers my conscience turned in the world of the hidden to obtain the likes of the angelic realm, and the unveiling of the secrets of might. My eyes moved around heaven as though I saw the gates of the angelic world; one of its chamber windows had opened. The Truth (glory be to him) faced me with the quality of beauty, and the beauty of his satisfaction appeared from him. My spirit flew to him, and the Truth was kind to it and full of expansive graces. He said, "What are you worried about? I am with you; I am the creator of all that is." Then he hid from me, and I remained in the delight of what I attained from him. When I awoke in the middle of the night, he appeared to me with the quality with which he appeared between the evening prayers. Then he drew near me, and the hidden aspects of his majesty and his beauty appeared. He snatched me from the gate of creaturehood, and made me fly in the air of his identity. Then I cannot describe my state, because after that station are ecstasies, visitations, and inspired speech, none of which enters into expression.

✸ 64. A Wine Poem

One day it happened that someone had invited me the previous night, after the later evening prayer, to an occasion for listening to music. The singer recited:

Does one appear in the morning with bloodshot eyes,
yet the wineskins' nostrils did not bleed?
Winebearer, relieve those souls
who have risen up with worries up to their collarbones.

Ecstasies, kindnesses, communications, and conversations from the station of expansiveness overwhelmed me, although there was nothing there except rapture, ecstasy, and certain gleams and illuminations. These moments and the encounter were adorned by that conversation with consciences.

✸ 65. The Station of Divine Laughter

When I settled down and departed, I meditated until the next day. I recalled these states until night came, and I performed prayer between the two evening prayers, and said to myself, "What was going on? The wonders of the hidden were not revealed in listening to music the night before." And I suddenly saw the Truth (glory be to him who is transcendent) at the windows of the angelic realm, dawning on me as beauty and majesty. And I said, being in a mood of expansiveness, "Where were you when you hid during the music?" And he who is transcendent said, "I was with you, as I am now, as you see me!" And I laughed and cried, and my conscience was glad, and my mind and heart. And I said, "My God, why did I not see you there?" He said, "I was behind you, and above you, watching you, and on your right and left, as you see me now." It was as though I experienced those events again, and as though I saw him as he described himself and manifested himself. And when half the night had gone, I stood and asked him to appear as eternal divinity, without clothing his attributes in actions; I implored him to do so. The lights of the essence and attributes appeared to me in the world of eternity in a likeness of oceans that filled one another. I saw splendor upon splendor, beauty upon beauty, glory upon glory. And I saw the ocean of holiness, and he manifested himself in the whole of it with the sign of satisfaction. It was as if he were laughing in my face with these lights. I learned that this was the station of laughter, and my conscience and my state at that moment were happy.

✤ 66. Beyond the World of Existence

The wonders of oneness manifested themselves to me, but the effects of the world of actions remained with me. I said, "My God, let me come to you by isolating your oneness from all else." Then he manifested to me the world of existence, rising like a full moon from behind the mountain peak, or like the sparks from a smokeless fire. And the Truth (who is transcendent) made me enter that world. I shed my skin of external accidents, but I could not stand apart from them, for that station is the station of sanctity, transcendence, and annihilation. He explained to me here the realities of reality, and my conscience was burned. It was said to me, "This is the world of oneness, which I have described in my book: 'There is no likeness unto him'" [Qurʾan 42:11].

⊛ 67. Divine Beauty in the Prophets

Then the Truth (who is transcendent) appeared to me, and he was beautiful. I saw Abraham in the mountains, and the stars of God's actions arose there; they are the mirror manifesting his essence and attributes. Abraham was seeking the Truth, and he was saying, "This is my Lord!" [Qurʾan 6:76]. Then I saw an awe-inspiring shaykh descending a mountain; he had reddened eyes, a mighty frame, and mustaches white as snow. I knew that he was Moses, descending from Mount Sinai.

⊛ 68. The Adoring Angels

I tried to explain my ecstasy and my spiritual state, and I recalled the angels and the world of the angelic realm in the beauty of my state. That world was unveiled to me, and I saw the spiritual, lordly, holy, majestic, and beautiful angels, sitting down and wearing the clothing of brides, more beautiful than I had ever seen them. I saw before me the "generous scribes" [Qurʾan 82:11] as though they loved me and longed for me, like beautiful youths in the semblance of drunkards, acting wary and fearful. I saw Gabriel sitting nearby, like a bridegroom, like a moon among the stars. It was as though he had two tresses, long like the tresses of women, and he was dressed in red garments with green silk trim, weeping for my sake and longing for me. In this way all the angels were happy to see me, as though they were my admirers, rejoicing in my state.

✿ 69. Vision of Family beyond the World of Thrones

Then I saw what I saw of the qualities of majesty and beauty, which the temporal is unable to comprehend. I reached a world where a hundred thousand thrones are smaller than an atom, and I saw nothing there but might and power. When I departed thence, I saw a great house high above, and I saw my family sitting and talking about me, reciting poetry; I felt a happiness like that of the first encounter. I saw all my womenfolk sitting happily, and I saw my children there, and a group of other people.

✿ 70. Mother and Father

Then I saw my mother, and she was a woman who knew and loved God; she stuck her head in my family's house and said, in the dialect of Pasa, "*Hi lillah walu,*" meaning, "There is no god but he." And they were recalling their weddings. Then I saw my father riding a red horse, wearing gold-embroidered clothing and a white turban on his head. With him were angels who came from visiting the Truth who is transcendent. He was an upright man, a lover of God—for God has his friends—and he was prone to weeping and was full of feeling.

✿ 71. "The Red Rose Is of the Glory of God Most High"

In the middle of last night, after sitting on the carpet of devotion in search of the manifestation of hidden brides, when my conscience soared in the regions of the angelic realm, I saw the majesty of the Truth in the station of being clothed with divinity, in the form of loveliness, repeatedly. It did not satisfy my heart, until from it came a revelation of the perpetual majesty that consumes consciousness and thoughts. I saw a face vaster than all of heaven and earth, and the throne and the footstool, scattering the lights of his glory, and it was beyond analogies and similitudes. But I saw that his transcendent glory had the color of the red rose, and it was world upon world, as if he were scattering red roses, and I saw no limit to it. My heart remembered the saying of the Prophet, "The red rose is of the glory of God most high." And that was the extent of my mind's comprehension. If at that time I had had one of the eyes of holiness, I would have seen him as he will be seen, God willing, with our own eyes on Resurrection Day, in all his eternity, glory, and primordiality, which are sanctified above the orders of time.

✵ 72. The Time of Descent

I was sitting one night at midnight, and the time of meditation became prolonged. I saw nothing, and none of the gates of the hidden were opened to me. So I wondered, and I became depressed, feeling this loss. I was distressed, and it occurred to me in my heart, "What have you to do with the descent of the Truth?" But this was the time of the descent, and I saw the Truth (glory be to him who is transcendent) as eternity. I became eloquent, raved, and entered ecstasy, and my heart's blood flew to my head. I viewed him with the quality of awe, magnificence, greatness, majesty, and beauty, until he came near from the world of the throne and the footstool. He displayed the brightness of his majesty on the throne, the footstool, and all the heavens.

✵ 73. The Removal of Doubts

Then he descended from the seventh heaven, and the angels fell before him. He halted for a while, and did the same in every heaven, until his blessing reached the heaven of the world. The light of his power comprehended everything. An hour passed, and he said to me, "Ruzbihan the leader [*makhdum*]!" I was filled with bliss by his majesty. He said, "Who is there who doubts that I am God?" Then he said, "Do you have any remaining doubt that I have unveiled this to you, and that I have chosen you for this station?" The subjects of evening conversations contain nothing like this.

❀ 74. Descent and Disappearance

Then God's light shone over the regions of the earth. I saw all the earth like the garment of divinity. I saw the transcendent Truth manifest from Mount Qaf to Mount Qaf. He appeared from Mount Qaf and all the mountains, and then he appeared from Mount Sinai, manifesting himself in the clothing of divinity, for some time. He bequeathed me these stations: first, love with oneness, and unknowing in knowledge; second, love with knowledge. He was kind to me, and his virtuous attributes appeared to me. Then he said, "This is my descent." Nothing temporal remains beneath the feet of eternal wrath. From where does he descend, and to where does he descend? All creation vanishes in his light and becomes smaller than a mustard seed in the sceptre of his magnificence. Then God said he was returning to the world of sanctity, for it was the time of hiding. Then I saw him as though he were hiding, bit by bit; then I saw him beyond everything, smaller than a seed. I abased myself, and my vision could not complete the witnessing.

❀ 75. The Prophets in Ecstasy

Then he appeared to me, as though I saw a carpet spread over nakedness, but Muhammad, Moses, Adam, Noah, and Abraham were not near him. I saw all the prophets and was standing among them, all of them in ecstasy. They moved and were agitated in longing, and spoke in rapture. I was like a handsome youth between them and the Truth. Muhammad and Moses (peace be upon them) were overwhelmed, and Adam chose to be naked, from longing. I never saw that in any other prophet.

❀ 76. Showers of Pearls

Then I saw above me an atmosphere of white light, from above which came showers of white pearls. They came from the beauty of the Truth, and he was scattering them on me. It is beyond expression, nor can intellects comprehend it. He then hid that world from me. Then I became occupied with the characteristics of these moments and those unveilings that I had forgotten. If any man or jinn saw an atom of these worlds, he would melt beneath God's sublimities—God transcends every description that is not worthy of his power.

❀ 77. "I Am Yours"

I saw myself being annihilated in the station of abasement. I said, "I am the least of your creatures; I am your servant and the son of your servant." And the assaults of oneness and might fell upon my heart, and he said, "Who are you that you should be a servant to me?" I became ashamed before God most high on account of what I said, and I said, "What should I say? For I am only one of the things in your kingdom." He said, "You will not be a true believer in one God until you forget yourself and all else besides me from the throne to the earth." I remained astonished in a great veil, and was unable to speak. Then I thought to remember him by reciting his names. He taught me of my annihilation in him, and my longing for him. He manifested himself to me in the deserts of the hidden, and he pointed to himself, saying, "I am yours." I entered into ecstasy, and my heart rejoiced. Then he approached in the form of the Turks, and my soul and my heart were annihilated in his beauty and loveliness. Then he approached me again and said, "You are not distressed by the word of oneness here, for oneness here is a ruse. You witnessed me as I was in the quality of beauty and loveliness."

✿ 78. The Station of Annihilation

Then he manifested himself in colors in the garments of beauty from every side around me, overwhelming me with passion, love, and longing, so that I found that my soul melted in the sweetness of my state. If I said anything of what I comprehended of the realities of unknown attributes, it would fill the world with divine realities. This is the station of the lovers who have drunk the oceans of oneness in primordial knowledge and the like, who are upon the ocean of greatness, the crashing of which bequeaths the unknowings of realities to the people of knowledge and love. They are in the station of annihilation; they have no eye that is not obliterated, no heart that is not dismayed, no intellect that is not annihilated, no conscience that is not vanishing. Glory be to him who transcends the allusions and expressions of all.

✿ 79. Swimming in the Oceans

I was seeking God most high in the hidden world. The more I sought him, the more intrusion there was from existence and from certain imaginings. I sought God's aid for that, and he made me comprehend his grace, and he expelled my conscience from the regions of existence. I reached the ocean of love, which was vaster than the world. I swam across that until I reached the ocean of knowledge, and I swam across that. Then I reached the ocean of mystical knowledge, and I swam across that, until I reached the ocean of oneness. I swam across that until I reached the ocean of unknowing and magnificence, and I swam across that until I reached the ocean of attributes. Then I reached the ocean of essence, and I was astonished that I lost the reality of the Truth. I settled down for some time. He appeared to me in majesty and beauty. All that I saw was related to his majesty as a drop is to the ocean. His kindness agitated me toward ecstasy and spiritual states. I remained there some time, and then he hid from me. It happened that I awoke later than my custom, and I was distressed by that.

❀ 80. Seeking the
Hidden Attributes

When I finished and sat in meditation, while I was thinking and speaking, my moment escaped me, and my heart revolved in the hidden world, seeking spiritual states, ecstasies, unveiling, and dialogue. I suddenly saw the Truth (glory be to him) as loveliness and beauty and glory, scattering red roses (glory be to his sublimities), so that I cried out and was in ecstasy for a time. Then he hid from me, and my consciousness traveled in the angelic realm until it crossed time and reached the threshold of might, but the beauty of the Truth (glory be to him) was not unveiled. I was greatly excited by perfect longing for God—"Every father's son is at his mother's breast." I waited for a long time. I abased myself, but I spoke expansively, for longing and love had overpowered me, because they motivate the action of lovers. I spoke certain words after experiencing that expansiveness and overpowerment, and the first dawns of attributes appeared to me.

❀ 81. The Tree of Turquoise

When the dawns appeared, they contained quantities of time, and I saw that all temporal things had been annihilated. Everything was as it was, and he (glory be to him) said, "The throne and footstool have disappeared," and they disappeared. Then he said the same thing of heaven, hell, the heavens, and earth. He said to Ridwan, "The inhabitants of paradise that day will be better in their home, and happier in their resting place" [Qur'an 25:24]. He meant by that their station. The world of paradises was revealed to me, and I saw something lovelier than that. I saw there the prophets, angels, houris, and castles, filled with the light of the Truth (glory be to him). Among the trees of heaven I saw the tree of turquoise, like a palm tree. It was putting out fresh growth, leaning forward and speaking. If the loveliness and beauty of this tree appeared to the people of the world, all would die of longing.

✸ 82. His Wife in the Garden

Then I saw my wife in one of the gardens in the presence of God (glory be to him), and she departed from him. And I saw the Truth (glory be to him) in the form of a Turk. Then I saw my wife in one of the upper chambers of paradise in the presence of God (glory be to him), and that upper chamber was of red ruby. My wife was sitting near the Truth on the side of a bench, as though she was waiting for me. Then I heard from the voice of the hidden the saying of the Most High, "With the righteous among their parents, and their spouses," [Qur'an 13:23]. So I thought about this message, and returned to the beginning of the verse where the most high says, "Gardens of Eden which they shall enter with the righteous among their parents, and their spouses, and their children" [Qur'an 13:23]. And I knew that this was good news for me, and at dawn I sat meditating on the daybreak of pre-eternity.

❀ 83. The Consolation of Beautiful Form

During this time, I worried in my heart about recalling my visual witnessing of God in the stage where he is clothed with divinity. I was concerned, because [the definition of divine oneness is] "the isolation of the eternal from the temporal." But the Truth appeared to me in the assembly of holiness, having likened himself, the Transcendent One, to a beautiful form with which he awakened the affection of his lovers. He drew near and said, "Arise, you are thinking of nothing." It was as if he hated my concern with his transcendence beyond imaginings. My heart rejoiced at his appearance in a form appropriate to the secret of my love. I remained in ecstasy, in a spiritual state until dawn, with sighs and tears. Then he himself appeared every hour in another attribute, from the qualities of eternal lights. Then he hid from me, and my heart pondered on the remembrance of my warning and preaching [against conceiving God in human terms] from the top of the pulpit. And he said, "My secret is what you have long preached for the guidance of the people, and my proclamation to them is the beauty of God's creation (glory be to him)."

❀ 84. Manifestation in the Pulpit

I saw the presence filled with the nearest angels sitting in the pavilions of splendor. I saw God (glory be to him) and all the prophets and messengers sitting in wait on the pulpit. When I sat [in the pulpit] and recited words of recognition, the angels wept, and so did the prophets. He (glory be to him) heard, and a light appeared from him with satisfaction, as though he agreed with them. God is transcendent. He said, "So it will be on the day of resurrection." My son, whoever imagines that these unveilings are the vague imaginings of God in human form will not attain union nor achieve results, though he scent the fragrances of sanctity and intimacy. These are experiences of holiness, the intentions of the sublime, and the stations of the masters of negation among the masters of perfection. The masters of manifestation recognize that these are lordly commands, appearances of the lights of eternity, and qualities of God's attributes by means of his actions.

✿ 85. Dawn on Mount Qaf

I awaited the daybreak of union, and an hour passed thus. I had an unveiling, as if I were beneath Mount Qaf and I saw a sapphire. The Truth (glory be to him) rose from beyond [the sapphire] and irradiated the world. I saw Mount Qaf and the earth that was joined to it dawning with the light of his majesty and his beauty, and he manifested his attributes and his essence. The earth quaked, and the mountains disintegrated, and that impressed me greatly. I awoke, and most of the night had passed, but nothing was opened to me of the angelic world except some visitations. When the time came for the call to prayer, I saw the Truth (glory be to him) facing me from the direction of the Little Bear, and he received me in the manner of union with him.

✿ 86. The Chamberlain of the Prophet

Then I saw him as though he were coming from the hidden world, and the stars of the Little Bear were seven rooms. [He came from] the hidden toward those rooms, and I saw that he had appeared from their seven windows. He appeared to me with the quality inspiring awe and respect. Then I saw many people coming from the direction of Medina. When I saw them, I saw all the prophets, messengers, angels, and saints. The Prophet was in the midst of these prophets and messengers, and his companions stood in front of him, and in front of the prophets were the Sufi masters. I saw among them al-Sari al-Saqati, and he was the greatest among them, like a chamberlain. He wore the robe of princes, with an outer garment of blue silk; upon his head was an ornamented hat, and in his hand was a bow with an arrow in it to drive people away from in front of the prophets. He was the chamberlain of our Prophet. They all came together. The Prophet stood beneath these rooms with all the people, and he raised his hand as though he were interceding with God most high.

✿ 87. The Loftiest Likeness

After midnight I saw him, the Transcendent One, as though he appeared in a thousand kinds of beauty, among which I saw a glory of lofty likeness, "for his is the loftiest likeness [in the heavens and the earth,] and he is the mighty, the commanding" [Qurʾan 30:27]. It was as though he were like the glory of the red rose, and this is a likeness. But God forbid that he have a likeness! "There is no likeness unto him" [Qurʾan 42:11]. Yet I cannot describe except by an expression, and this description is from the perspective of my weakness and incapacity and my lack of comprehension of the qualities of eternity. In the river bed of pre-eternity there are deserts and wastelands in which dwell the snakes of wrath. If one of then opened its mouth, none of creation or time would escape. Beware the one who describes the pre-eternal Lord, for in the oceans of his oneness all spirits and consciences are drowned, and they vanish in the sublimities of his greatness and might.

✿ 88. A Son Designated God's Representative

I was with him in a thousand assemblies of expansiveness, and he was with me in a thousand assemblies of affection, until he loved me, with his loveliness and his beauty. This sweetness remained in my soul. Then I saw him, the transcendent, when he appeared, and I was concerned about one of my sons. It was as though he approached him and made him stand and was kind to him, saying, "This is my representative." Then he dressed him in the robe of the great ones, and then he stopped. The proximate angels were with him. Then he conveyed me to the heavens of eternity, until from the gate of greatness he brought me near, and when I looked at the world of greatness, I saw nothing in these worlds except radiant shining lights. I could not look at them, because of the extremes of the flashing lights of greatness. I saw a white world with mines in it, and that was the presence of the Almighty, and I saw that it was empty of people.

❁ 89. The Smallness of Creation

There I saw the Truth (glory be to him), approaching me as if he wished to bequeath me himself and caress me. When I saw him, my conscience boiled with longings for him, but I did not draw near him, because of his great majesty. I remained an hour, then I saw [him] in the world of eternity in his greatness and sublimities. Then I saw him in the form of Adam, and in my heart I thought this was the secret of oneness. Then he manifested his hand, and I saw something in his hand like a tiny ant, and I did not know what that was. He said, "This is the throne, the footstool, the heavens, the earth, the nadir, and the zenith." Then the word of the most high inspired me, "They do not measure the worth of God in truth, for the entire earth is in his grasp on the day of judgment, and the heavens are furled up in his right hand; glory be to him" [Qur'an 39:67]. I remembered the saying of the Prophet, "Creation in the two hands of the Merciful One is smaller than a mustard seed."

❀ 90. Possessing the Throne and the Footstool

He appeared to me as majesty and beauty, then he abandoned me in the station of love. He hid, and when I sat in the station of meditation to trap the birds of the hidden, I saw the Truth (glory be to him who is transcendent) between the throne and footstool with a beauty and majesty that cannot be described. The throne and footstool were like two treasuries whose doors he opened. Then he closed them, for they are both places where secrets are found, except for certain of his lovely attributes. And he said with the tongue of eternity, "Are not both of these [treasuries] yours?" At length he ravished my heart with the grace of his creation, in unveiling his beauty and majesty, until it made me in the likeness of a madman from the rapture overwhelming me. It increased my longing for him, and I was happy in his beauty and his grace toward me. Those hours passed by me.

❀ 91. The Bridal Canopies of Intimacy

He hid, then he displayed to me the bridal canopies of intimacy. He turned me through veils of majesty in the realm of majesty. I saw [him] among all his bridal canopies and among all the veils, and I saw the assemblies of intimacy in these bridal canopies. I sat on all the carpets, and he showed himself in the loveliest of qualities. He wined me with the wines of nearness, and in that place I was like a bride before God (glory be to him). What happened after that does not enter into expression. Glory be to him who transcends the reference of everyone who reduces God to abstractions and the expression of all who see him in human terms.

❀ 92. Manifestation Without Quality

I saw him in seventy thousand of the stations of unveiling, then I returned to my attributes. The knowledge of his attributes and the knowledge of his essence that remained to me was smaller than a mustard seed. My spirit, heart, intellect, and mind were in the oceans of knowledge, unknowing, sanctity, transcendence, eternity, and divine presence, in astonishment at the greatness of annihilation. Glory be to him, the one who shows himself to those whose quest is weak in accordance with their own qualities. But he transcends change in his singleness and cannot be encompassed by creation. I was watching God most high, awaiting the unveiling of attributes and the lights of the essence, and the Truth (glory be to him) manifested his eternal face to my heart, without me asking how; it was as though I was looking at him with an external eye, and the hidden world shone from the appearance of his glory. Then he appeared and hid, repeatedly.

❀ 93. Prayer of the Prophets

I saw a great light from the direction of Medina. A quarter of the sky and the earth was seized and joined to that light, and when I saw that I knew that that light was the light of Muhammad (peace be upon him). It was in the midst of an awe-inspiring light. I could not look at it for its overpowering majesty and awe. I saw in front of the light one of my companions giving the call to prayer. He was great in size, dignity, and impressiveness. Then I saw Adam and Moses and all the prophets giving the call to prayer in front of the light of Muhammad, praying toward the presence. When Muhammad arrived at "the praiseworthy station" [Qur'an 17:79], I heard the Truth (glory be to him) say to him, face to face, "Muhammad! One is one," alluding to his oneness, and the annihilation of all else besides his power.

❀ 94. Roses of the Prophet and Consuming Majesty

An hour passed. Then I saw Muhammad (peace be upon him), seated in the upper chamber of the presence. He was the red rose. The glory of red roses was blazing from his face; his tresses were unveiled. The Truth (glory be to him) was manifest in this form. He called me and named me by my name, saying, "Ruzbihan!" The light of his greatness and the sublimities of his transcendent face consumed a thousand miles times a hundred thousand miles, all of creation, and none could reach him. This is an allusion to the assaults of his majesty, which cause time to vanish at the instant it first manifests itself.

❀ 95. Caresses and Removal of Doubts

Then God drew me near to him, and opened for me the room of union. I was like a child in the room of his mother. He caressed me with the caress of the beloved for a lover. Then the crashing of the oceans of oneness seized me, and he annihilated me with his powerful greatness. The Most High said, "It is I; do not doubt me. The mighty Lord is your God and the God of all creation. Are you worried about the likeness you thought of? That is the vision of me and the unveiling of my majesty to you." Then I saw myself in the land of God most high, and in the cities of the hidden. I saw in every place the unveiling of God most high in the clothing of beauty and loveliness. When he returned me to the world of the hidden, he made me see what he made me see.

❀ 96. The Window of Eternity

Then I saw paradise and the houris, castles, trees, rivers, lights, prophets, saints, and angels that are in it. I saw the figure of the

Truth, as though there were a window from the world of eternity. I saw the Truth (glory be to him). I said, "Let me know about paradise." He said, "People of paradise! I come every day seventy thousand times to this window from the world of eternity, and I look upon paradise with longing for the meeting with Ruzbihan." His transcendent face was full of majesty and beauty, and paradise was filled with loveliness and intimacy. I was happy because of that, with a happiness that nearly made my heart fly away with my body. I saw that ecstasies had overwhelmed me, from the subtlest visitation of the hidden. Those were the first steps toward witnessing.

✤ 97. Lullabies from the World of Jewels

Then the beauty of the Truth (glory be to him) appeared to me in a lovely form, so near to me that no veil remained between us, nor any distance. With all love, he caused something to appear to me from the beauty of his attributes, which stole away my tranquillity and my peace. He placed me in the station of intimacy and the joy of the spirit, and the second half of the night passed me by. I was between sleeping and waking, and he appeared to me in a world filled with the jewels of holiness. He who is transcendent was among these jewels in the form of Adam, wearing white clothes, and he talked to me and spoke to me and was kind to me and lulled me to sleep, until another hour passed.

✤ 98. "Two Bows' Lengths or Nearer"

Then I worried, thinking about my spiritual state, and when I prayed two cycles of prayer, I expected the manifestation of the lights of the hidden, and the shining of the glory of eternal lightning. And I saw the Truth (glory be to him) in the form I saw him in between sleep and waking, as though he were in my house. Then he approached me until I was hidden in him, then my thought recited, "He drew near and came down, and he was two bows' lengths or nearer" [Qur'an 53:9]. Because of this I was taught ecstasy, intimacy, sobriety, and intoxication. I remained in that state until dawn, and witnessed a witnessing, the manifestation of which was like the red rose. And he called me and said, "Do not the ants go bearing all my secrets away from me?" The hearts of the ants are filled with the graces of his secrets. This is a saying in which is the manifestation of wrath, greatness, and might.

❁ 99. The City of God

I was seeking the Truth (glory be to him) after what happened, in terms of ecstasies that have no cause except in longing and agitation. Such longing is acquired when the lights of manifestation touch the innermost consciousness. He does not appear to intellects except by what separates them. The doors of the hidden were opened. I saw oceans white as pearls, between which was a strip of land. I saw the Truth (glory be to him) on the strip of land in his perfect beauty and loveliness. He brought his face near to me, gracefully and affectionately, and I remained there for hours in ecstasy and unveiling. Then he was in a great city called the City of God most high, and I reached that city in seeking the Truth. I saw there nothing but the signs of his existence, but no visual unveiling was unveiled to me. Then I saw God most high wearing the garment of majesty. He called me and approached me in a way that I cannot mention. I remained witnessing him, like a loving and maddened son.

❁ 100. Dancing with the Truth

One day I fell into the oceans of longing, and the crashing of the ocean of greatness took me to the station of witnessing divine presence. I saw the Truth (glory be to him) unveil to me his beauty and majesty as the lightnings of his face's sublimities. I remained gazing at his beauty and was utterly intoxicated. I nearly gave up my spirit, my intellect nearly vanished, my heart nearly flew away. My conscience was annihilated, but my form remained in the ecstatic joys of witnessing him. He turned his face toward me as though the delights of his highest majesty appeared and ravished my mind. At dawn I saw that the world was filled with the Truth, and I was in a state both hidden and present, as though I saw him and as though I did not see him. He came then, and his dancing excited me, so I danced with him. I remained in that moment and state until sobriety arrived.

❀ 101. "Do Not Worry"

Prior to that I was in the station of longing and agitation, and before that I was concerned about concentration. He spoke to me with advice, saying, "What are you concerned about? Do not worry." Though he is in every thing, the reality of God's existence transcends conceptualization in the heart of any of his creatures. Between the evening prayers I saw myself fall into the presence. I saw its lights and the expanse of the kingdom of the angelic realm, and I watched the unveiling of eternal beauty. And I saw the Truth (glory be to him) in majesty and beauty in the pavilion of the presence, approaching me in a way that I cannot express. And I fell after that in the oceans of oneness, and I saw him after that repeatedly, every hour, in majesty and beauty and glory.

❀ 102. States Like Thunderbolts

Then most of the night passed, and I saw the Most High coming; he received me from the throne and the footstool, and he manifested himself as he did to Adam in paradise, and to Muhammad at the lotus of the boundary after the great witnessing. When I saw him in that condition, states like thunderbolts descended upon me, from the effect of the sublimities of his face. He did not hide until I passed away in him, from my pleasure in him. Then he hid and appeared suddenly in a form of the most perfect loveliness, beauty, and majesty. He took my tranquility away until an hour had passed, then he seized me and set me turning in the kingdoms of the hidden.

⚙ 103. The Longing of the Masters

He took me while I was in a state of nearness to him, and he caused me to enter the veils of the hidden, until I was hidden from the hidden. When I departed, a moment passed. I saw myself as though I were in Shiraz, and the doors of heaven opened, until I saw the throne and the footstool. I saw the master Abu ʿAbd Allah Muhammad ibn Khafif and all the masters separating and gathering, as if they were anticipating that the Truth would summon me there. The Truth (glory be to him) manifested himself to them, and they were sighing, moaning, and crying in that moment, and all of that was from their longing for me.

⚙ 104. No One in Between

Then he manifested himself in a special way, with no one between us. He said, "You will see me from a space of three hundred thousand years." An hour passed, and I saw the Most High facing me from the hidden as if he were making me hear a music from within himself, which I cannot describe. I melted in that moment from his sweetness, not finding anything more delightful than him. Then I saw the Most High in my house, "in the most beautiful form." I cried out and wept, and I drowned in oceans of nearness. Then he approached me until no distance remained between us, and I was sitting by him. He said to me, "I long for you utterly." I said, "My God and my friend! When I come to the time of my departure from this world, take me yourself and let me enter the veils of the hidden with you." The Most High said, "So it will be." Then I hid from him. After that it was the time of the morning call to prayer. Praise be to God who chose me in pre-eternity for these great degrees. He is transcendent, and when he reveals himself in the expected places for witnessing him, his being does not change with the changes of time. In every account of him, he adapts to the states of those who describe him, though he is as he was in pre-eternity, not circumscribed by the qualities of time.

❁ 105. Between the Throne and the Footstool

I wondered at his manifestation between the throne and the footstool, and I thought, "He transcends the throne and footstool and all of space." When this thought occurred to me, I saw the throne and the footstool by his noble face, as though they were dust, and they were annihilated by the awe of his majesty. What I have told you, my friend, is the stopping place of the knowers of God during the descent of God. The arena of his attributes transcends resemblances to time.

❁ 106. The Transcendent Face

I saw him in the depth of the night, after my longing for the meeting with the Truth (glory be to him) became perfect. I saw gardens with rivers in them, and the Truth (glory be to him) sitting by the river bank. He turned his face toward me, and I saw the joy of satisfaction in his beauty. I was in a state of rapture and intimacy, unable to contain myself from doing the things that a rash drunkard will do when overcome by recklessness and joy, and he does deeds of both kinds. Then he hid from me, and I saw him afterward standing with attributes of beauty, ravishing his heart with love. Then I saw him standing, manifesting himself to me the beautiful attributes that ravage my heart with love. I saw him at the door of the hidden, and his face was wider than the seven heavens, the seven earths, the throne, and the footstool. Everything is perishing in his transcendent face [see Qur'an 28:88]. Brother! This and the like of it none knows but the lordly, the eternal, the majestic, the holy, the angelic, the mighty. The Most High says, "None knows the interpretation of it except God and those rooted [in knowledge]" [Qur'an 3:7], because the symbolic verses are reserved for the hearts of love. One who does not love eternal beauty does not know the unknowable aspects of the attributes in God's actions. God is beyond the expression of all who understand God in human terms or reduce him to abstraction.

✦ 107. The Ranks of Angels

My heart heard from the criers of the hidden his saying (glory be to him) "By those who are set in ranks, those who drive away with reproof, and those who recite a remembrance" [Qur'an 37:1–3]. I considered the meaning of the verse, but I did not know what God most high intended by this speech. I saw the presence filled with angels as though made of hyacinth and ruby, standing in rows like Turks before sultans. So I knew the meaning of the saying of the Most High, "By those who are set in ranks." Then I saw the Truth (glory be to him) reveal to them lightnings of majesty, beauty, glory, and greatness. If every atom from the throne to the earth were a tongue for me, I would be unable to describe the Most High, from his perfect beauty and loveliness. When he manifested himself, some billowed over others, some were raised above others, some eclipsed others, and some drove others away, from their overwhelming longing for God (glory be to him), for they wished to be near him. So I knew the meaning of his saying, "Who drive away in reproof." When they approached him, they were overwhelmed by intoxication and rapture, and the words of drunkards ran off their tongues, like boasting, ecstatic expression, and unknown expressions such as I say in ecstasies of intimacy. And I knew the meaning of his saying, "Those who recite a remembrance." That is the station of awe in intimacy, and happiness in love, and longing in sweet union.

❀ 108. The Descent of Manifestation upon the Mountains

When an hour passed, I remembered in my heart the matter of descent. I saw the Truth (glory be to him) clothed with divinity, in beauty and loveliness, sitting on the roof of my lodge in Shiraz, with me rapturous before him. Then I thought of the secret of union, the realities of singleness, and the holiness of power. The Truth (glory be to him) looked at existence. I saw all the mountains fall before him in prostration and then disintegrate. The throne, the footstool, all the heavens and what they contain, and the earth and what it contains, all fell in prostration. Then I saw him, and he made me realize that his manifestation with that attribute was a mercy and kindness to me. I remained between intoxication and sobriety and oneness and love. I saw in the midst of these unveilings all the mountains coming near to the Truth (glory be to him), and with each one of the mountains was a drink of holiness for me. I was very happy. Then I thought, "What listener possesses these secrets, so that I may tell him of the magnificence of their degree?"

❀ 109. The Orchard

It happened that I bought an orchard near Pasa after the death of one of my wives, and I thought, "How can I seek a livelihood through the orchard after her death?" I heard the crier of the hidden say, "[The inhabitants of paradise are] happier in their resting place" [Qur'an 25:24]. I thought about the verse and realized that the statement was the saying of the Most High, "Depart" from the garden, as al-Malik [the angel in charge of hell] said, "Depart" from the fire. Anything but God most high is annihilated in less than an eye blink. The Truth remains unveiled in the beauty of oneness and the power of endlessness. He said, "Everything is perishing but his face" [Qur'an 28:88]. That is the station of singleness and annihilation. I remained astonished and was annihilated, and I do not know where I was.

❀ 110. Oceans Like Air

Then he hid from me and made me enter oceans like air, which had no dimensions. The might of the Truth encompassed me. I saw myself in these oceans like a drop, with no left or right, no before or behind, no up or down. I saw nothing but glory upon glory, power upon power, majesty upon majesty, might upon might, greatness upon greatness, eternity upon eternity, post-eternity upon post-eternity. Then he said from the wombs of the hidden, "This is endless eternity and eternal divine presence."

❀ 111. In the Form of Adam

After that happened, I saw myself as though I were above the seven heavens, with the angels and prophets sitting like brides. The Truth appeared as beauty and glory, and he passed by them. They all sighed and wept for his loveliness and transcendent beauty. God was clothed with the clothes of beauty in the form of Adam. It appeared to me that those angels were standing by his door, waiting for the unveiling of his majesty, at every moment and with perfect longing, and this is their eternal custom. The Truth (glory be to him) descended to the earth and went round from east to west, then approached me and said, "I came for you when you were asleep." He then stayed in my house an hour, in a form I cannot describe. But I found my heart and body melting at the sweetness of seeing and witnessing his beauty. He said, "Seventy times I came to seek you from the wombs of the hidden before I created you, and I visited your places for you, though between me and that were regions, the hidden realm, deserts, and oceans, a journey of more than seventy thousand years." Then he approached me until he drew near, and drew near, and again drew near, until I was hidden and annihilated. God is beyond every imagining and indication and expression.

❀ 112. The Transcendent Secret

This is a spiritual state, and its secret cannot be stated. It consists of the secrets of lordliness, the making of the attribute, and the appearance of graces. His sufficing mercy and his bountiful blessing arouse affection in his servants who are knowers and lovers; but for his favor, how would they comprehend the lights of the sublimities of his face, when they keep company with the accidents of time? If he appeared with the perfection of his power, all existing and created beings would be consumed. Do not be concerned, my friend; unveilings like these have descended upon most of the prophets and upon the sincere ones, but they have only reported and preserved them through expressions of being clothed with divinity. He transcends anyone conceiving his essence and attributes in terms of the attributes of individuals.

❀ 113. Calling the Angels to Prayer

I saw myself after midnight in an unveiling as though I were in Shiraz in my lodge. I looked toward the prayer niche and saw God (glory be to him) manifesting himself and appearing more beautiful than I had ever seen him. From his majesty and his beauty he appeared satisfied, but he hid from me, and I remained in the depths of ecstasy and spiritual states. An hour passed, and I saw the Most High on the roof of the lodge, facing the direction of prayer and giving the call to prayer. I heard him say, "I testify that Muhammad is the messenger of God." The earth was filled with angels, and when the angels heard the transcendent Truth call them to prayer, they wept and sighed and could not keep themselves from coming nearer to God most high, from his magnificence and greatness. In my conscience the saying of the Most High was recited: "They fear their lord from above them and they do what they are ordered" [Qur'an 16:50].

❧ 114. The Drums of Authority

I saw the Most High frequently as though he were playing the lute at the door of the lodge. Happiness and joy seized the world until all things laughed, atom by atom. I saw the Most High frequently before that, above every above, playing on drums himself. By that he indicates that he does this to display my kingship. He selected me in my time for kingship and succession to rule over the world. This and similar things are examples of the display of election, acceptance, being chosen, and true union. The Most High transcends what the hearts of cherubs and spirituals think, and what the hearts of mortals think. These are the manners of his favor to the saints, and there are many similar things in prophetic sayings. How is this related to the saying of leader [Muhammad] of the messengers, the prophets, and the saints? Anyone who thinks that I am to be doubted, after the display of these unveilings, is a fool who has not scented a single fragrance of the ecstasies of the saints and the raptures of the Sufis, by which they understand the symbolic prophetic sayings. He [Muhammad] said, "God most high will show the form of his essence in the way that he wishes."

✿ 115. Tasting Union

I saw him between the two evening prayers, while I was in the station of reproach and expansiveness. I saw the pavilions of the angelic realm as flashes of longing reached my heart. Most of the night passed, and I sat in meditations, lifting my thoughts above my heart. My conscience flew through the worlds, but I could not pass beyond the realm of existence, because I did not see anything beyond existence that was unconnected with that power. So I returned to my place, until some time passed. I saw the house of the brides, which is the house of majesty. The Truth appeared by himself to me, and he made me enter the station of expansiveness and ecstasy and spiritual states, tasting union with him. I never tasted the like of it. He wanted my longing and my love. Then he approached me with a nearness I cannot describe. I was concerned at first about the disappearance of the sanctity of oneness. He said, "Walk around me, the Truth." He taught me that the station of love means abandoning the people of the attributes while forging intimacy with the people of the essence.

✿ 116. The Music of the Spheres

I sought God most high at dawn, but I did not find him. He created in me spiritual imaginings in different forms, turning them into the thought of oneness and making them familiar with the thought of love. Time passed, and all my concentration was on the occurrences of lights of special manifestation qualified by eternal attributes. These do not give rise to the shapes of actions or the qualities of being clothed with divinity. But the Truth manifested himself first from the womb of the hidden, then from the throne, and then in the form of Adam. My concentration learned from this, and it sought the reality of oneness. He manifested himself to me with attributes and with beauty that I cannot describe. But I will say some of what I saw of him when he manifested himself; pearls and roses scattered from his face. I saw him in a world full of shining planets, and the Most High was as though he were displaying musical instruments. All existence laughed from the pleasure of it. Then he manifested attributes every instant with an attribute more beautiful than I had ever seen. That was his artistic creation, in his spontaneity.

✽ 117. The Likeness of Beauty

I saw the prophets before God (glory be to him) raving and roaming. I was seeking the Truth by being reticent about his oneness while proclaiming his attributes. Whenever wonders of the hidden appeared to me as shapes, I rejected them, until I saw the Truth (glory be to him), without asking how, in majesty and beauty. He pointed, and there were mines of lights. Then I saw him at the door of the country of eternity, in the enclosures of pre-eternity. When I met him in majesty and beauty and greatness, I drowned in oceans of ecstasy and spiritual states; the agitations, sublimities, and motions were in accord with the states of intimacy. Then I was astonished in the primordiality of the Truth, and I saw him in "the most beautiful form." I thought in my heart, "How did you fall from the world of oneness to the station of symbols?" He came near and took hold of my prayer carpet, saying, "Stand! What are these thoughts? You doubt me, so I made a likeness of my beauty in your eye, so you would be familiar with me and love me." There were countless lights of majesty and beauty upon him. Then I saw him every moment with a different beauty.

✽ 118. The Clear Victory

After I performed ablutions, the beginning of this experience was my being spoken to by the beloved. He said, "We have granted you a clear victory, so that God may forgive you for your sin, for that which is past and that which is to come" [Qur'an 48:1]. When he drew near at dawn, he ordered me to perform devotions. I said, "I did not achieve my wish from you; by your power, feed me the food of your love, and show me the realities of your beauty and your majesty, so that I may take joy in you and melt in you from the sweetness of intimacy with you." He said, "Stand and go up to the roof of the lodge; there will be unveiled to you your desire." When I went up and gave the call for morning prayer, I saw Shaykh Abu al-Hasan ibn Hind in the station of meditation. I said to myself, "What do you want?" A voice sounded in my inner consciousness, "He is meditating on majesty." When I looked, I saw all the Sufi masters, from the edge of Turkistan to the far west, meditating on his majesty.

❁ 119. Dancing like a Drunkard

I saw Muhammad with all the prophets and messengers sitting in meditation on the witnessing of God's majesty. I saw Gabriel and all the cherubs meditating on the witnessing of holiness. Then I saw the Truth (glory be to him) manifest himself to them as I described, and I among the Sufis was like a raving drunkard, bringing my face near his power. He approached me and made me dance, and danced with me, and chose me for that from among them. When I tasted the sweetness of expansiveness, I was overwhelmed by the shouts of the angelic ones, the cries of the eternal ones, the moans of the lordly ones.

❁ 120. Muhammad in the Deserts of the Hidden

I was in search of God most high in the deserts of the hidden. I saw Muhammad on the paths of those deserts; his stature is the stature of Adam, and he was wearing a white shirt and a pure white turban. His face was like a red rose, radiant with smiles. His face was turned toward the world of eternity in search of the Truth (glory be to him). When he saw me, he drew near me; we were like two strangers in the desert with a single destination and purpose. He was kind to me and said, "I am a stranger, and so are you; come with me in these deserts so that you may seek God (glory be to him)." So we walked on the path for seventy thousand years, sitting at certain places to eat and drink. He fed me and treated me kindly, like a stranger dealing compassionately with another stranger. When we approached the curtain of eternity and the pavilions of pre-eternity, we waited for a long time, and did not see the Truth. We were concerned about his absence. Then the transcendent Truth appeared to Muhammad, and I saw him show something to him. I was looking at God (glory be to him) and how he dealt with his beloved. Time passed, and secrets occurred between them of which I was unaware. I thought in my heart that I saw them both, and they both have accepted me.

✤ 121. Beyond the Deserts

The Truth (glory be to him) took me and showed me things in his hidden world, causing his love for me to appear from all of himself. Then I saw lights, majesty, and beauty, until he showed the deserts of the assaults of oneness. We passed beyond them, where there was no place for us to stop, because when time draws near to the power of eternity, it ceases and is annihilated.

✤ 122. A Feverish Son

It happened one night that I was concerned on account of my son Ahmad, who was suffering from dysentery. This distressed me, and I asked my beloved to make a substitution [for my son's illness]. I slept while Ahmad did, and awoke at his shout; I came to him, though I was between waking and sleeping. I saw a person leaving from the side of my house, saying in Pasawi Persian, "May your night be a safe and blessed night." Then he said [to my son], "Tonight he descends for your sake and for the sake of your father. The Truth, he, is yours." I said to myself, "I was distressed at this time, so how will the unveiling be prepared for me?" I pursued the verses of good news from the Qur'an, which announce the opening of the gates of the Hidden. For that reason, some [divine] speech causes action and some inspires.

❀ 123. Scattered Jewels

At dawn the doors of the angelic realm opened, and I saw oceans and a heaven of glistening jewels scattered over my head. I saw God (glory be to him) as though he were scattering those jewels over me from that world. He displayed the form of satisfaction, as majesty and beauty. A dense light shone from him like those jewels. When certain graces and kindnesses occurred, and time passed, I saw that heaven rolled out on the face of the earth. I saw all the prophets, saints, and angels, and the Truth (glory be to him) manifested himself to me from among them. He said things to me that I heard, words of the station of intimacy and expansiveness, and of his longing for me and his passion and love for me.

❀ 124. The Face of God

The face of God most high, transcending the indication of thought, was unveiled to me. I hid [from] the faces of the Living, the Substantial One, who is most high and holy. He manifested himself within me, and from the vision of his face came the sweetness of longing, the melting of the spirit, the agitation of the inner consciousness, the shattering of the heart, and the annihilation of intellect. If an atom of this befell the mountains of the earth, they would melt from sweetness. I was sighing, weeping, turning, and sobbing. God took me into the angelic realm, and he placed me at the door of eternity. Then he manifested himself to me as greatness and magnificence. I saw light upon light, glory upon glory, power upon power, and I cannot describe it. I was unable to proceed a step closer because of his majesty and power. If I looked at it forever, I would be unable to understand an atom in the likeness of any of his pre-eternal qualities. But God is beyond anyone's description.

❀ 125. Descent to the Human

I saw in some of my unveilings an idol in the center of the world, glittering with light, and this upset me and provoked me to draw near to the Truth (glory be to him). When an hour passed, I saw the pavilion of the hidden, and the tents of the angelic realm were opened. The Truth appeared to me (glory be to him) as power, divine presence, majesty, and beauty. He appeared to me himself, and he taught me the hidden aspects of his character. I saw a glory and loveliness from him, and his light revolved between heaven and earth. I saw him, and I was facing in every direction. Then he showed me the fields of oneness, and I entered them. I was snatched by the storm of the sea of oneness, and it drowned me in the ocean of primordiality. Then he returned me to human creation. I was concerned about the humility of descent into humanity and worldly limitations, worrying about some of my affairs, the persecutions that had happened, and how beginningless eternity became measured into time. But I became glad, my nature left me, and my inner consciousness shed the trials of hidden events.

✤ 126. Annihilating Everything but Him

My spirit saw a shining light in the center of the angelic realm. The Truth arose from the light with the loveliest of attributes, the most beautiful beauty, and the greatest majesty, coming up to me with his transcendent and holy face, saying, "How can one who negates any creature restrict himself to anything but me?" I remained in his majesty and beauty, and that is the state of the nearness of nearness, and the union of union. That state remained until he annihilated everything but himself from my thought and my conscience. I remained there, in the essence of the essence, and the reality of reality. The Truth appeared to me and for me in the form that I mentioned. He bequeathed me his nearness, and he unveiled his majesty, his beauty, and his speech, in a marvelous place and a perfect ecstasy, with sighs, tears, raving, bewilderment, dancing, clapping, and whirling. My intimacy, my longing for him, and my love for him increased.

✤ 127. Those Who Know the Symbolic Verses

I settled down after that until dawn, and the Truth was unveiled as I have described. For a long time I witnessed the cloaking of divinity in oneness, the manifestation of God's attributes in action, and the projection of lights of his essence in unknown attributes. When the time of sunset drew near, I saw the Transcendent One heading toward the most hidden of the hidden. I saw the people of the gardens and the angels and prophets of the presence rising with him to their places. I did not see at first, but he made it clear to me that when God most high descends (in the sense of acceptance, not movement), the inhabitants of the angelic realm descend with him; when he lowers the veils of power, they are hidden with him. These unveilings distinguish the masters of negation among the knowers of God, and they qualify the realizers of truth among recent masters, whom the Truth has placed on the level of knowing the decrees of the symbolic verses [of the Qur'an]. These are the ones whom God most high described as "the firmly rooted" in his transcendent saying, "None knows the interpretation of [the symbolic verses] but God and those who are firmly rooted in knowledge" [Qur'an 3:7].

❀ 128. The Dress of Beauty and Majesty

I awoke at midnight on the first of Ramadan. The Truth (glory be to him) spoke to me with his saying, "Their lord will give them good news of his mercy and acceptance" [Qur'an 9:21]. After praying two cycles, I sat in meditation and thought about the blessings of God and his verses. My conscience roamed through the regions of existence, and my spirit departed from existence. The Truth (glory be to him) appeared to me beyond creation, as though he came from the hidden, wearing the dress of beauty and majesty. His character was such that the influence of his majesty and the unveiling of his beauty would melt all existing and temporal beings that beheld him. By God! I wanted to describe some of his attributes that I saw, for my disciples and sincere ones, but I could not do it, because the Transcendent One appeared in the form of a garment in which Adam was hidden. He displayed it to the cherubs and spiritual beings, and "They fell prostrate before him" [Qur'an 12:100] involuntarily [as his parents did to Joseph]. Thus the Prophet said, "God created Adam in his own form."

❀ 129. The Brilliant Lightning of His attributes

Understand, were it not for fear of the ignoramuses who accuse us of making likenesses of the cause, I would have indicated something of what I have seen of the Truth (glory be to him): the light of his glory, the brilliance of his holiness, his great majesty, and his gracious beauty, and the qualities with which he clothed himself, and with which he clothed Adam, Moses, Joseph, Abraham, John, and Muhammad. By these qualities, of which they inherited the most luminous, they stand above the world and its creatures. When the brilliant lightning of his attributes manifests itself in something, all existing, temporal beings submit before it; it emanates from the quality of pre-eternity, and here there is no separateness, connection, imagination, or fancy. He who knows God most high after traveling in the world of eternity knows the unknown sciences that reveal the lordly secrets, by which the consciences of the unified ones are purified of denial and assertion, beyond understanding God in human terms or reducing him to abstraction. These things are existing times, and he, the Most High, is beyond that. Fancies are annihilated in the journey of the knowing spirits to these meeting places, and when they reach there, they know nothing, even though their hearts think of the cause of existing beings. For the vision of the Truth has nothing to do with proof or cause and effect. The Truth (glory be to him) appeared to me in the station of intimacy, with a lovely quality and graceful beauty. He seized my heart with his beauty, and I was overwhelmed by cries, sobs, tears, clapping, ecstasy, intimacy, longing, passion, raving, affection, and love. Then he hid, and I abased myself, begging to meet with the Generous One. Then he appeared to me in a quality that is foremost in the symbolic verses; then he hid from me.

✵ 130. Utmost ʿIlliyyin (I)

Grace seized me and made me fly in the air of ʿIlliyyin. I saw the gardens [of paradise] and those who reside there, and the dwellers in the presence, who have the bodies of angels. I saw the Prophet Muhammad with all the other prophets, with the appearance of Sufi masters, whose hair and mustaches were of snowy white, with white garments and white head scarves. They were calm, settled, and dispersed through the deserts of utmost ʿIlliyyin, each one of them facing the divine might from his station, moving toward it. I was in the dress of a youth with a robe, wearing a hat, with my hair in two long tresses. In my hands was a lute, and I was facing the Truth. I saw a group of my own masters sitting on their prayer carpets, including Junayd, Ruwaym, and Abu Yazid al-Bistami, with a group of masters facing towards the presence of God most high. Junayd amidst the Sufis was like a full moon among the stars. Then I saw a group that had come from beyond the garden. When I looked at them I saw my masters and companions. Then a crier called, "These are the people of my district."

✵ 131. "You Took Her and Left Me Wild"

Then I traveled to the door of the presence, and the Truth appeared to me, facing me with his majesty and power. I saw greatness, magnificence, majesty, power, divine presence, and glory, with creation and time set in their midst. Then I saw a purse in which were things like mustard seeds, and I did not know what it was. A call came in my conscience, "These things are the throne and footstool and the gardens, and all creation from the throne to the earth, in the deserts of the hidden, crumbled and split up, small as the head of a pin." I remained astonished, without knowledge, heart, or spirit. When I awoke at the first dawn, I was concerned, since I slept more than I [usually] did every night. Then I thought in my heart of my wife who has passed away (may God have mercy on her). When I performed ablutions, I said in my thought, "My God! Do you see what you have done to me, when you took her and left me wild?" He spoke to me in Persian and said, "Doing that is not to be done." He meant by that that he nearly unveiled to me the world of the angelic realm and made me dwell there [he nearly had me die also]. So I understood that. Then after ablutions, God spoke to me, saying, "Rejoice in the bargain you have made" [Qur'an 9:111].

❀ 132. Drowned in the Oceans of Longing

When I had prayed two cycles, the Truth welcomed me to the valley of pre-eternity, and I was a stranger there. On the heights of greatness God appeared to me as majesty and beauty. Then he showed me the hidden world; for that reason I was afraid of [having missed] the call to prayer of the muezzins. I said, "I have wasted my day, and I did not awaken soon enough." The transcendent Truth told me, "Do not worry; even if you were asleep, I was with you and was not asleep, but was being kind to you and raising my veil to you." Then the Most High showed himself repeatedly in a way I cannot explain, and he drew near to me in the form that I loved. I was drowned in the oceans of longing, and raved in the assemblies of intimacy. My heart was between veiling and manifestation, my spirit between ecstasy and nothingness, my intellect awaiting lordly commands, my conscience witnessing might and the angelic realm, my tongue describing eternity, my eyes on the turning of the angelic realm, burning with tears, until the Truth (glory be to him) witnessed me in the form of sweet union, and I witnessed the Truth with unveiled majesty and beauty.

❈ 133. Entering the Door of the Presence

One night it happened that I received an assurance of a way to God most high. The transcendent Truth spoke to me, saying, "Your effort is meritorious" [Qurʾan 76:22]. I learned that he had established for me certain unveilings of the hidden as an achievement. When I sat and hours passed, I passed, in my concentration to the outer portion of the angelic realm. I saw a group of angels and prophets (peace be upon them) standing at the door of the presence, on both sides of the presence, standing like princes at the door of the angelic realm. I saw the scholars and jurists beyond their rows, and I saw al-Shafiʿi in the dress of the jurists, handsome of face and form, with a shawl. He went behind the row, and he recognized me between the lines of prophets and angels, though he was like a stranger there. I entered the door of the presence and was hidden from human agency. I saw the Truth (glory be to him) beyond seventy veils, with face unveiled in majesty. Then I entered the abode of majesty and saw the Truth (glory be to him) in seventy beauties and majesties and glories. I saw nothing with these forms except what God wished. Then I entered the realm of power and saw the veils like roses, and they were white roses. I saw the Truth (glory be to him) among the white roses clothed in the glory of the white rose, and he was unveiled there. Then the transcendent Truth called to me in the world of the cosmos, saying, "My beloved ones! No one loves him." Then he arose and called out, and named me by my name, so I loved him. Then he showed me the special nearness that he had singled me out for, among all humanity on the face of the earth. And during those hours I was to the saints like a king among princes, and like a red rose in spring among all the fragrant herbs, all in rows, in ecstasy, reddened and drowned in tears. But he had entered the deserts of the hidden.

✻ 134. The Tree of Red Roses

I saw the Truth (glory be to him) by a tree of red roses in majesty and beauty, and I was standing by the tree. I saw our Prophet with red and white roses in his sleeve, and he poured out the roses from his sleeve, and so did all the prophets and angels. I saw Adam, and he had a rose, and I saw Gabriel, and he had a rose. The Truth (glory be to him) approved of them being thus. Then the loveliness of the attributes and the beauty of the essence appeared to me in the attributes of the actions. Then he unveiled to me the veil of power so that I entered into the veil. I saw his magnificence, majesty, power, and divine presence. Eyes, hearts, intellects, spirits, and consciences are astonished at this, but God transcends every expression and allusion. The remembrances of drinking at the fountains of love descended on my heart. My conscience was agitated by this kind of longing [to perform] the rituals of the birds of nearness [prayer]. I remained there between raptures and ecstasies until between the evening prayers. I thought about the essence of divinity, preparing for the approaches of pre-eternity. The assaults of power appeared with this quality, and their assault attracted me away from the affairs of humanity. Sublimities and unveilings continued to reach me, until the Truth (glory be to him) appeared on the steed of pre-eternity, with a Turk's bow in his hand, and he was angry at people who persisted in hunting his servants. I saw ʿAli ibn Abi Talib (may God ennoble his countenance) come out from a mountain enraged at those people, and he attacked them, for some of the oppressors were his descendants. Before this chastisement they had oppressed the devotees, but the rights of their houses were not abrogated. Time passed, and I was between ecstasies witnessing visions, and each witnessing had a different attribute. Night passed, and only half of it remained. The Truth (glory be to him) appeared to me and came near my side. I saw him in his loveliest attributes, in the most perfect beauty and the most graceful majesty. I saw him appearing from the gateway of power and the veils of eternity, and he manifested his majesty as though he were filling the world with red roses, which is the light of his glory. He called, saying, "Whose is the kingdom today? It belongs to God, the One, the Conqueror" [Qurʾan 40:16].

✿ 135. Fragrances of Ascension

I sought God the transcendent on certain nights, and I saw him arise in my house in majesty and beauty. He showed himself (he is great and mighty) as he never did to the nearest angels. Then he hid, and abandoned me in ecstasy and spiritual states. Then the Truth called from the world of eternity, summoning breezes, and he ordered them to bring me to the land of pre-eternity. The fragrance of his realities seized me and made me fly in the air, and so on, until seventy thousand fragrances seized me, each one a vehicle of the hidden that God most high has numbered for his ascensions. I reached the Truth (glory be to him) and saw him as holiness, glory, power, might, and greatness. He spoke, and called me by name, "Ruzbihan, have you seen any dimension, form, imagination, or likeness?" I thought silently that this is the station of oneness, and all of time and what it contains was annihilated.

✿ 136. The Saints of
Pasa and Shiraz

I saw myself in a graveyard in Pasa, and saw a saint leave his tomb wearing red clothes, with a red hat on his head. When he stood, all the masters of Pasa stood with him. Then they came with me to Shiraz, and when we drew near Shiraz, all the masters of Shiraz arose from their tombs to welcome us until we reached the town. This was in a time when I intended to return there. I saw myself on the eastern side, and the Truth (glory be to him) manifested himself to me in pre-eternal beauty, and my heart melted from his extreme beauty and loveliness.

✤ 137. The Loveliness of Turks

After an hour I saw God manifest himself to me, and he manifested the loveliness of the Turks. They gathered in the desert of the East before God (glory be to him), and when he manifested himself to them, they were amazed and "fell prostrate before him" [Qur'an 12:100] from their perfect longing for the majesty of God most high. Then I saw myself sitting down and resting, and God recognized me, and he told me that he had walked all over the world seeking me, seeing no one else worthy of witnessing him. When he hid from me, I saw that he was wearing a tight garment. I had hair on my head, and a hat. The Truth drew me from the wombs of the hidden power and I approached him, taking the form of an arrow shot by a powerful bow, or a speeding spear. Nothing, not sea, wind, mountain, heaven, nor earth, opposed me. I pierced through everything above and below it until I drew near him.

✤ 138. Scattering the Angels
   like Butterflies

I saw the Most High without place or dimension in the world of power and magnificence, the same way as I saw him in the East. When he manifested himself, the angels gathered in the pavilions of his greatness in the form of Turks wearing red clothes. The Truth (glory be to him) manifested himself to them and they became enraptured and bewildered, scattered like fluttering butterflies. I expired in pleasure at the beauty of the most high Truth. I did not expire like that except according to God's will. I saw in the world of the throne the witnessing of God most high in the form of majesty and beauty and glory, suddenly, after I sought the goals of the secrets in different regions. What I was with him was what God wished. I entered the oceans of ecstasies and joy, witnessing him in the station of intimacy. I was hidden from him for a time. He removed the veil of pride from in between, though there was no in between. I saw him in that form, and he drew me near kindly, displaying affection and acceptance, and said, "Welcome, Ruzbihan." I cried out in joy, I clapped, I hummed. I learned from him that he was mine, and time passed. I was hidden from him. I implored him to let me expire in pleasure from him. Time passed.

✸ 139. "Am I not Yours?"

Then he opened another world after the throne, above the footstool, in a realm where dimension was not even discussed. The Truth was unveiled to me in the form of sublimities of power that manifested themselves. I flew from my place to him, and he said, "What are the ambitions that have occurred to your heart? Am I not yours, and am I not sufficient for all your ambition? I am vastly liberal and generous." I remained in the beauty of witnessing him, chanting and singing with delight, announcing his divine presence, his majesty, his beauty, and the loveliness of his creativity. I hid from him, and my joy was endless.

✸ 140. Revelation beyond Miracles

I sought union with him another time. It happened one Thursday night that I recalled with my companions the realities of secrets. I said to them, "One who gets revelation from the most high Truth does not do so unless he is an angel, a prophet, or a saint. Revelation comes from God after unveiling and witnessing. The angels have a form that, when manifest, allays suspicion on sight, and the prophets have evidentiary miracles that on appearance remove doubt regarding the truth of the prophets' revelation. The saints have charismatic miracles; when their miracles occur, no doubt remains about their revelation either. I am not in these three categories, for I am not one of those who perform charismatic miracles. My purpose is to reveal the truths of knowledge and the rare divine sciences that God most high has chosen me to receive, which through the manifestation of the most high Truth taught me by a word of a station beyond the station of charismatic miracles." The Truth (glory be to him) spoke to me on Friday night while I was in those states that I have mentioned, saying, "Have you learned that I was sitting with you last night by your side in the form of majesty and beauty? My face was beside yours, with a mirror in my hand reflecting my face and your face. I was looking at your face, and looking from your face to the mirror in which both our faces appeared." It was as though I was looking at the glory of the Truth (glory be to him). I cried out and shouted repeatedly. I wept and implored his perfect grace and extreme generosity, so that he placed himself in the garments of his power, so that he himself saw me. For he knew that time is unable to confront eternity and the sublimities of pre-eternity during the display of oneness and eternality. In the beginning of the dawn of his majesty, time and space vanish like the feathers of a bird in the fire of Abraham. He transcends all thought and whatever is thought in the heart of any of his creatures.

✤ 141. Reflecting the Beauty of God

I experienced a moment of witnessing from intoxication and sobriety, wearing the clothes of brides, with tresses on my head like the tresses of women, with unveiled head and breast, like a beautiful king emerging from the bridal bower among his boon companions. I saw myself flying in the angelic realm, and I saw all the people of the presence, but I saw none with the physical beauty of my form. It was as though they fluttered toward me in longing and love, but I did not abide with them, but kept on flying to the meadows of spirituality, until I reached the Truth (glory be to him). I looked at him and then looked at my face, and his beauty was mine, and my beauty was his. I was in the position of an intimacy indescribable by any creature of God (glory be to him). That is where the divine has his nature and his oneness.

✲ 142. The Ocean of Blindness

I dived into the ocean of blindness seeking the vision of the Truth (glory be to him). I raised my head in the ocean of astonishment and saw a world of greatness, and I saw nothing but greatness upon greatness. I was in awe of it, and I returned. I saw in a desert the Sufi masters, cloaking their wives with the woolen shawls of the monastery. Then they put them down and spread them out. I saw among them red rose petals that they appeared to like. They did not get excited like others from the world of nearness, on account of the wrath of this magnificence. I saw among them Shaykh Abu al-Hasan ibn Hind, Shaykh Jaʿfar al-Hadhdhaʾ, and Shaykh Abu ʿAbd Allah ibn Khafif. Then I sought the Truth after that for long hours. The Most High welcomed me, wearing clothes of glory, silk with pearls and red gold. Upon him were lights like sashes of white pearl and red gold. He clothed me with loveliness and beauty, in a place of beauty that houris of the gardens of paradise would melt from seeing.

✲ 143. The Pleasure of His Beauty

I saw him with that form another time on the road, and that was in one of the valleys of the hidden. Then ecstasies of longing overwhelmed me, and I asked the Most High to increase my vision of him. So I saw him, and I could not bear it. I said in my thoughts, "Ruler of the heavens and the earth, what can remain with you if I see you, when I have expired in the pleasure of my heart from your beauty?" It happened that I attained my goals of unveiling attributes and manifesting the essence, and my conscience traveled through the regions of existence and existing things, seeking exit from time. I saw myself as if I were on the roof of my lodge in Shiraz. I looked up and saw the Truth (glory be to him) in our market in the form of majesty and beauty. By God, if the throne saw him in that form, it would melt from the pleasure of his beauty. I entered the oceans of ecstasy, spiritual states, and gladdening visitations weighed with longing, love, and passion. Then I saw myself sitting on the patio of the lodge, and the Truth (glory be to him) came in that form with even more of his beauty, and with him were how many red and white roses! He cast them in front of me, and I was in the station of intimacy, happiness, and the spirit was in a place such that I melted. When the beauties of his attributes and admirable qualities were unveiled to me, then he hid from me.

✸ 144. Utmost ʿIlliyyin (II)

I rose up in an hour to the utmost ʿIlliyyin. I saw the prophets, saints, and angels standing in ranks, some of them seeking the nearness of the presence. They wore the clothing of awe. I hastened toward him in longing, weeping, raving, intoxicated. I put my head on the pavilions of splendor, and the blood dripped from my eyes over my flushed face. I found no one more humble to him than myself. I was in extreme need of union with him. We all went back together, and we did not grasp an atom of the lights of his power. We remained astonished, and I sat in the stations of astonishment and abased myself. My conscience plunged in the oceans of imaginations, and I rejected all of them from the battlefield of my thoughts. I was there until the witnessing of holiness was unveiled to me in the form of laughter, and here creatures and time laughed from the pleasure of that laughter.

❀ 145. The Night of Power

I had thought about the distinction of the Night of Power, the eighteenth night of Ramadan. It was a divine custom with me, that he showed me the Night of Power every year. Sometimes he gave me a revelation after afternoon prayer, and sometimes at the time of evening prayer, with the two verses of the Night of Power. He showed me the signposts and what they will contain regarding the shapes of the world of the angelic realm, prior to their occurrence. I said in my thoughts during prayer, "God! Do not restrict me from the vision of the Night of Power." I saw the regions of the heavens opened as far as the utmost ʿIlliyyin. I saw in it the cherubs and spiritual beings, as though perplexed from their descent to the world. I saw the crowd in the gardens, and Ridwan ordered the houris of the garden, and he saw them henna their hands and feet like brides. I saw some of the angels take drums and bugles and military instruments. I saw at the door of the presence of God most high (glory be to him) Turkish drums, and they were about to beat them. I saw red roses about to be scattered from all of the presence of God (glory be to him) over all the world and the people. I saw the prophets and sincere ones separating and gathering. I saw the Truth (glory be to him) about to unveil himself to all creatures in the form of glory and majesty. He revealed to me that the Night of Power is the twenty-first night. It is the custom of the cherubs and spiritual beings, when they bestow the Night of Power along with Gabriel, that they laugh and rejoice. Sometimes I saw them like Turks, and sometimes I saw them like brides with the tresses of women, with the faces of beauties. I saw some of them in the form of gazelles, and I saw no angel more beautiful of face than Gabriel. I sought God (glory be to him) at dawn on this night, and he spoke to me as he spoke to Moses there [at Mount Sinai], and several mountains split open. I saw in Mount Sinai a window in the mountain itself on the east side. The Truth (glory be to him) manifested himself to me from the window, and said, "Thus I caused myself to appear to Moses." I saw Moses as though he saw the Most High, and he fell from the mountain, intoxicated, to the foot of the mountain. I saw a witnessing of grace more lovely than this witnessing.

✸ 146. The Tears of Regret

One day I heard the story of some of the Qurʾan reciters and officials who wrote against the ecstatics and realizers of truth among the knowers of God, the masters of oneness among the unveilers, and the sincere ones among the witnessers. They attacked the claim of the masters and their spiritual stations. I was pained at that and asked God most high to forgive them for what I heard from his saying, "Compensation for calumny is to ask forgiveness from those who are offended." Then I prayed the evening prayer, and I saw a yellow dog in the deserts. I saw all the slanderers with their mouths open, and the dog with his tongue was pulling the tongues of every one of them out of their mouths, and he ate all their tongues in less than an instant. I finished with that, and it was the night before the twentieth of Ramadan. Someone was saying, "This dog is one of the dogs of hell; every day its food is the tongues of slanderers, and the fasting of anyone whose tongue is eaten by this dog is unacceptable to God most high." I sought help from God from his punishment, and wept and implored him. Then I thought, if slander brings this reward that I have seen, what is the reward of this weeping in regret?

Then I saw angels with beautiful faces coming and picking up my tears and drinking them, saying, "We are those who fast for God most high, and we break our fast with your tears." Then I saw the Prophet coming toward me from Medina, in the fearsomeness of a Turk, wearing a robe and a hat, and his right hand was sticking out from his robe, and he had a bow and some arrows in his left hand. He opened his mouth and took my tongue and mouthed my tongue gently. Then I saw Adam, Noah, Abraham, Moses, Jesus, and all the prophets and messengers coming toward me, and they mouthed my tongue. Then I saw Gabriel and Michael, Israfil, Azraʾil and all the angels, and they mouthed my tongue. So [did] all the saints and sincere ones. Ecstasies overwhelmed me, and cries and sighs. Then God most high in the form of majesty and beauty lifted the veil of the angelic realm, unveiling in the form of Adam the qualities of the attributes. Then he showed me his magnificence and majesty in another station, and so on, until I saw him in seventy stations; he was in each station as I saw him before that, in exactly this character. He spoke to me a magnificent speech. I responded to him in every speech. Then he made me sit at the table of bounty. I saw upon him the colors of his magnificence, the like of which never occurred to me in my heart. Then the most high Truth drew me close, away from those things. I said, "God, you transcend eating and drinking. When I cried from regret, the angels drank my tears. What will they do with my weeping from longing and intimacy in witnessing?" He (glory be to him) said, "That is my wine." This is one of the laws of his grace with the prophets and saints, for he transcends the attributes of time.

❀ 147. The Hungry Guest

Have you not seen how he said to Moses, "I will be your guest for a meal." And Moses prepared to receive him, and he awaited the lovers of the Truth (glory be to him) from his sure faith in the word of God most high. A poor man came, and he begged from Moses rudely. Moses said, "Take a jar and fill it with water from the Nile, then come and eat what you wish." The poor man disappeared, and the invitation of Moses was not fulfilled. The Israelites ate what was on the table, and then Moses returned to Sinai. He said, "My God and master, you did not fulfill the appointment." The Most High said to Moses, "I came to you and asked for food from you, and you sent me to the Nile." He said, "God, you transcend the like of that." The Most High said, "Moses, don't you know that when you feed the hungry poor man, you feed me?" So it is stated in the prophetic sayings.

❀ 148. "The Merciful One is Sitting on the Throne"

Then I saw the Most High in the form of greatness and eternity and divine presence, repeatedly, then I saw him in the majesty of intimacy in the form of holiness where no station remains. I dived into the oceans of eternity and pre-eternity and post-eternity. Then I was annihilated of all my attributes, and I descended to the world of the angelic realm. I saw all existing things, compared to his power, smaller than a mustard seed. Then I went to the fields of pre-eternity intoxicated and raving, and he clothed me in the clothes of his loveliness and his beauty. Here I was the beloved of God most high, and he (glory be to him) loved me and was kind to me with kindness that none of the creatures of God most high could bear to hear of if I mentioned it to them, except as God wills. Then he bestowed on me his attributes, and he made me assume his essence. Then I saw myself as though I were he, and I remembered nothing but myself. I halted at that point and descended from lordship to servanthood. Then I desired the station of passionate love until I saw myself in the abode of majesty. I saw the Truth (glory be to him) arrayed in the form of divinity, and I remained in the station of intimacy for an hour, hidden from all that is other than him. Many ecstasies overwhelmed me, with agitation and weeping for the station of intimacy, and applause for witnessing with the eye.

He called me repeatedly, and I prostrated myself then and saw on my back the weights of the lights of magnificence. I said, "God, what is this?" He said, "The light of the 'sitting.'" I asked him, "What did you mean by saying, 'The Merciful One is sitting on the throne'?" [Qur'an 20:5]. The Most High said, "When I manifested the throne, and my manifestation takes place from the throne to whomever I wish, that is my 'sitting' upon it." This, my brother, is the story of the masters of negation among the knowers of God. Anyone who is not in the place of knowledge and looks at this book will accuse me of giving God the form of a man, but his head will be cut off.

✺ 149. Astonishment on the Night of Power

It happened by the grace of God most high on the Night of Power, the eve of the twenty-first of Ramadan, that on that night I saw marvellous shapes. Among them I saw angels in the form of Turks, some in the form of brides, and some on top of Mount Qaf. I saw some playing drums, and at the door of the presence I saw Gabriel singing with musical instruments like a boy. All the people of the presence were overwhelmed with happiness and laughter, and they descended from the mountaintops to the desert and the valleys as though they were celebrating together because it was the Night of Power. God most high manifested himself in the first part of the night, and in the middle of the night: in the first part of the night from the wombs of the hidden, and in the middle of the night from the utmost ʿIlliyyin, as though the Most High manifested himself from the red rose. I saw nothing lovelier than him in all these unveilings. Then he descended toward the end of the night arrayed in the form of divinity, majesty, and beauty, with the Prophet before him. He said, "You were only guided to my nearness and my witnessing according to my wish. If I wish mercy for anyone, I open for him one of the doors of the hidden. But they do not dare approach me, because my nearness is the nearness of mystical knowledge, not the nearness of distance. What distresses you? I sustain with my essence, with no before, no distance, no after, no below, no right, no left, no imagination, no fancy, no nearness, no distance. Glory be to me! I am pre-eternal, post-eternal, without time; I exist, I am powerful, eternal, without place. Substances are astonished in the realm between the throne and the earth, and nothing remains in their hearts but astonishment. You too are one of the astonished ones. There is no oppression upon you."

✸ 150. The Demand for Union

I said, "My God, I am not satisfied with that." And it was as though I saw him and did not see him, for I was in a kind of blindness. Then he took the veil off that blindness, and I saw him in the inner world of the hidden, but still I did not see him as I wished. So I implored him; I saw him in the outer world of the hidden, and I did not recognize the reality of union with him. I became angry and pained and said, "It is right that your servants turn away from your door and face inward to themselves as their direction of prayer. What is this distress?" I remained for a while, and I saw the Most High, and he appeared in the outer world of the angelic realm. I saw him in the form of majesty and beauty, and he drew me near and I approached, and it was as I wished, but I could not bear the extreme ecstasy, spiritual state, cries, sighs, and disturbance from his overwhelming loveliness and beauty, and the sweetness of union with him. I remained in that state for a time.

❊ 151. Time and Eternity

Then my heart asked, "How does he treat existing things and time, and how are they related to his magnificence and might?" I saw the face of the Truth (glory be to him) in the form of magnificence, and it was as though I nearly melted; I saw existing things in stormy winds. The beginning of this unveiling was that on this night I saw in a dream certain unveilings of the garment of divinity. When I awoke, the Truth (glory be to him) spoke to me and said, "[Zulaykha] said [to Joseph], 'Go out to the women,' [and when they saw him, they praised him]" [Qur'an 12:31]. When I saw him, I praised him, and he said, "How good is the wage for the workers [who dwell in paradise]!" [Qur'an 29:58]. Thus I learned that God (glory be to him) would appear to me and give me what he gave the prophets and the pure ones. But when I witnessed him with the witnessing of the stations of hidden journeys, I was astonished at the degree of God most high with his saints, and I wondered at their union with him: How could it be? For time is time, and the eternal is eternal. What relationship do they seek from him? I halted above him, next to him; his perfection seemed to have lost the credential of oneness.

❊ 152. The Stations of Moses and Muhammad

But then he manifested to me the rays of the dawning suns of the attributes, and my heart rejoiced. I saw them as if it were a station nearer than any I had ever found granted by the Most High. My mind recalled the story of Moses. I saw him seek nearness to the Truth (glory be to him), his vision of him, and certain lofty stations and noble miracles, as is handed down in traditions. My thoughts vanished, and I said, "God, you transcend relationship with creatures. You gave to Moses these miracles and these stations, and you chose him for perfection. What is the relationship between you and him, in terms of nearness? I too am from the sons of Adam; What have you given to me?" And he manifested himself to me in the form of majesty and beauty, and said to me, "Moses came to me, but I came to you seventy thousand times between the time you lay down and the time you woke up. Each time I removed the veil from your face while you were sleeping, and I awaited your awaking." When I heard that, I was swallowed by crashing waves of the oceans of oneness.

When time passed, he hid from me, and my heart flew in the world of the angelic realm and ascended above every above, and the essence manifested himself to me with the lights of magnificence and majesty. Then he said, "Have you not read in the Qur'an, 'He, God, is one; he, God, is eternal; he did not beget nor was begotten, and there is no one equal to him' [Qur'an 112:1–4], and 'There is no likeness unto him' [Qur'an 42:11]? Have you seen anything of existence, have you seen space, have you seen time, have you seen form, have you seen anything of temporal causes or existing beings? It is I, you see me in the form of majesty, power, and divine presence. This is the world of oneness, and this is the station of oneness."

I remembered the stations of our prophet Muhammad (the blessings of God upon him), when "he drew near and came down" [Qur'an 53:8]. Was there in his witnessing anything but the witnessing of holiness? God (glory be to him) revealed to me the moment when he himself brought him [Muhammad] by night to the station of being clothed with divinity. Muhammad said,

I saw my lord in the most beautiful form. He said, "Muhammad, what does the highest assembly of angels debate?" [see Qur'an 38:69]. I said, "What, lord? You are wiser." So he said it another time. And he put his hand on my shoulder, and I felt the coolness of his fingertips upon me. Then I knew what was, and what will be.

So goes the prophetic saying. And I learned that God most high graced me when he showed me the stations of oneness and the stations of love that the prophets saw. This was his mercy, for I sought him in the form of eternity and the quality of greatness in every moment. He taught me that the station of oneness and the station of being clothed with divinity are necessary to the creeds of the people of love and oneness.

❀ 153. Request for a Witnessing

I was sitting in the office of meditation seeking union with reality. Remembrances accumulated and thoughts followed, and I fought with devils and rejected their representations, and time passed. Nothing was opened to me, and I gazed at my conscience, and my heart was heavy, from the bitterness of loss. I remembered God most high in absence and presence, and talked like the people of expansiveness, saying, "What is this closing and opening? Your gift will be opened up in the hidden if you would only manifest yourself to me with the eye of oneness. Who in heaven and earth would stop you? If you grant me the witnessing I request, after unveiling your majesty and beauty, who would scorn you, who would attack you, who would dispute with you from the throne to the earth? Are you not the Lord of the heavens and earth? The changes of time would not harm you. You are safety, safety, the one whose saving grace is sought; what you do to your saints and the people of your longing," I said, using words from the conversation of the people of expansiveness and intimacy, "is something that the infidels, in their extravagance, would not do to the faithful." So he placed me in my desire, in the lights of the manifestation of the essence in the attributes, and the manifestation of the attributes in the actions. He appeared to me every hour in the garments of lordship, in the actions of something that the Sufis call the station of being clothed with divinity. Now every time I saw him, I sighed and cried and clapped my hands, and my conscience and intellect were glad, and sought him by isolating his oneness. Whenever he saw me after that, eternity strode forth from the wombs of pre-eternity to the heights above existing beings and time.

❀ 154. The Call of the Crow

I awoke one night contrary to my custom and was concerned that I had done so. I was extremely tired in the middle of the night, because I had not rested that day, and I started shaking. Hidden causes shook me, but I did nothing. Someone was saying, "I long for the remorseful one;" it was one of the verses I had heard from singers. I knew that this was nearly the time for a message, but I did not reach it for an hour. Some people knocked at the door, and then I knew that the Most High wanted me to get up. I arose and performed ablutions and said to myself, "The night is gone, and dawn is passing; how can I meditate?" I feared that the doors of the hidden would not be opened for me. Then I heard the call of a crow, and it was a pretty note, and loud. That message in the crow's voice was not what I expected at that time. But I knew that God (glory be to him) had opened for me one of the doors of his treasures of generosity.

❀ 155. The Hand of God (II)

I prayed two cycles, and sat in meditation. My heart dived into the oceans of actions, but I found nothing but blindness upon blindness. Then I dived and reached the world of chosen actions. Then I crossed that and reached the lights of the wastelands of the attributes. There I was between veiling and manifestation. The most high Truth (glory be to him) manifested himself from the world of power, and I said, "What is this manifestation?" He said, "Manifestation through magnificence and greatness." I remembered that and looked, and there the hand of God (glory be to him) was revealed to me. I saw from the wombs of pre-eternity to the world of post-eternities an endless light, as though he had with his hand seized all beings and time into a ball. Time was nothing outside his transcendent hand. The Most High spoke to me, saying, "The hand of God is beyond their hands" [Qur'an 48:10]. I was not satisfied with these unveilings, and I thought about the sublimities of beauty. My mind considered the saying of the Prophet, "His veil is light; were he to lift it, the sublimities of his face would consume as far as his eye could see of his creation." When I thought of that, the lights of the sublimities of his transcendent face reached me, and I was nearly consumed by the action of God most high.

❀ 156. Sitting with the Truth

I saw our Prophet, Adam, Noah, Moses, and the great prophets. I was adorned by separate sublimities, and I remained with them. God seized me with pre-eternal power, and he unveiled to me the majesty of his transcendent face. I saw time from the throne to the earth as though it were manifested without his face, and it was like the smallest mustard seed. The Truth (glory be to him) spoke to me, saying, "Everything is perishing except his face" [Qur'an 28:88]. This put me in the oceans of ecstasies, and I was like a moth in the rays of the mighty sun. The Most High bestowed upon his servant what he desired, and I knew that sainthood is a pure gift. I asked God most high for knowledge. I finished prayer, and then the Truth (glory be to him) sat with me in the form of majesty and beauty, and he intoxicated me with the wine of his union, he ravished me with the perfumes of his intimacy, and he increased my longing with cups of his expansiveness. I went into a beautiful ecstasy for a time, and I demanded from the Most High a clear manifestation of his attributes and the perfect holiness of his essence. When I saw him in the abode of majesty on the carpet of nearness, my longing for him increased, and I wanted him to share with me his beauty and union.

✿ 157. Rolling in the Deserts

Time passed, and I wanted from him a witnessing greater than this. I saw the Most High in the deserts of the hidden, and I saw myself rolling in the dust before him in these deserts, and I rolled before him from the first desert to the last desert, more than a thousand times. The Most High was looking at me with the eye of magnificence and majesty. Then he said, "Thus did Moses, rolling in the dust with no clothes on, five times a day, humbling himself before God most high and submitting to his might." God transcends the journey of the thoughts of the sanctified and the concept of those who proclaim God's unity. He is in the form he himself has described in pre-eternity and post-eternity. My conscience flew in time, and I saw it all, empty of the eternal essence and attributes. God transcends space and time. I said to myself, "If the like of these existing beings and time existed now, as existence, then their like would exist forever, above and below, to the right and left, before and behind. This is God most high, who transcends all space and time and [any] incarnation. Where will one seek God, and who will see him, if God does not want to manifest his essence to him? He is in his essence in pre-eternity and post-eternity." I was astonished by seeking, and when I saw him in the form of majesty and beauty in my house, in the most beautiful form, I was ravished, in love, and in longing, and my love and affection increased. In my ecstasy and spiritual state my heart did not remember arguments about understanding God in human terms or reducing him to abstraction, for in seeing the Most High, all traces of intellects and sciences are erased.

❀ 158. The Blood of the Substitutes

Time passed, and I saw him again, and he arose from the hidden in the form of majesty. I remained in the danger of ecstasy for hours. Then I saw him at dawn and he appeared in the form of majesty and beauty and power and glory in the deserts of the hidden at the door of the presence. I plunged at the crack of eternal dawn into the blood of the Substitutes, and he manifested that to me, and I was dyed in the blood of the Substitutes. I said to myself, "Who am I among them? Perhaps I am one of them." I saw him dyed with something more delicate than that dye, above their dye, and he indicated that that was my blood. I went into ecstasy from joy, and cried out repeatedly. My conscience, heart, spirit, intellect, and soul nearly flew in the air of selfhood, and became nothing in the lights of knowledge with that. I feared from what I saw that this would lead to a calamity, for I saw the Most High in one of my past experiences as though he were sacrificing and pouring my blood in the ditches of the hidden, and afterward I fell into a great calamity. I asked him for help then, and said, "I take refuge with you from you." Then I saw myself in the abode of majesty on the carpet of intimacy with the Truth (glory be to him), and he offered me a wine I cannot describe. I reached the station of union, intimacy, and beauty—may God nourish me and you with these lofty stations for ever!

✸ 159. The Movements of Sacrificial Victims

It happened to me on the night before the twenty-ninth of Ramadan, between the evening prayers, when taking care of certain worldly matters. Suddenly joy, shaking, intimacy, and longing fell upon my heart, and they agitated me with movements like the movements of sacrificial victims already made drunk, and my speech was like their intoxicated speech. Then after that, the Truth (glory be to him) was unveiled to me, and he said, "How long will you be concerned? I will do as you wish." That was after he drew near to me and was in the form of majesty and magnificence. He remained with me for hours. Then he manifested himself to me from the world of the angelic realm, and he manifested himself continuously to hearts annihilated from pre-eternal and post-eternal attributes. He called me repeatedly, and all my sorrow departed. In witnessing him, I was overcome by closeness, expansiveness, love, longing, passion, ecstasy, sighs, and tears. But I wanted more clarification of sublime eternities. So he spoke to me, saying, "God has given a value [*qadr*] to everything," [Qur'an 65:3], and I understood from that things such as the ambiguity of the rites of the Night of Power [*qadr*]. Then I passed most of the night, and I awoke, and was in my meditation, chanting.

✸ 160. The Flight of the Spirit

I saw the Truth (glory be to him) from one of the windows of the angelic realm in a form that would have melted all creation from sweetness and pleasure. He spoke to me and was kind to me again and again. I remained thus until the time of the call to prayer. The doors of the hidden opened, and my thought traveled in the form of thought and time, seeking the beauty of the Merciful, who is exalted and sanctified. But my thought was not able to traverse existence, because it reached the limit of time by knowledge, not by witnessing, and beyond that it saw nothing but blindness and imagination. It did not perceive anything of the lights of sanctity, and it suffered, returned, and hesitated for a long time. The Truth (glory be to him) appeared in the form of beauty, and he put me in his vision with perfect longing for his nearness and union. Then he hid and I implored him to return. He appeared in the form of majesty, and made me bewildered and passionate with his transcendent countenance. Then he abandoned me and hid, and the sweetness of witnessing him (glory be to him) remained in my heart. The scents of the breezes of holiness spread through the station of intimacy, and the light of awe filled my heart, as though the Most High were next to me in the form of greatness, suddenly. My thoughts and heart were confused, my spirit flew, my intellect fled, my secrets were refreshed, and my ecstatic moment was joyful. He displayed to me the light of his glory.

✸ 161. Drowned in the Oceans

I saw the Truth (glory be to him) in the form of power, and I understood nothing of him. When I saw him in the world of the hidden, he illumined from the angelic realm the expanse of kingdoms with the light of his majesty. He manifested a form I cannot describe, and was facing me directly (glory be to his majesty) as though he were standing and making the hidden aspects of the attributes and the beauty of the majesty of the essence appear. Then the oceans of the sublimities of his face pulled me in and drowned me in them. After that I did not see the lights of greatness; I returned and fled from them, for understanding is cut off there. The taste remained in my heart, and this witnessing remained in the eye of my spirit, as though I were seeing him as I saw him all the time. He bequeathed that vision to me in intimacy and agitation, and I was in the period of contraction, joined to sorrows, piling up the wrath of loss, until the Truth (glory be to him) awakened me in the form of nearness in majesty and beauty, and I hid in the oceans of ecstasies. Then the Truth (glory be to him) appeared to me in veils of manifestation, and before the Most High was every kind of angel, accompanied by candles made of spiritual beings, until they reached me. I was undone repeatedly by the manifestation of his majesty, but he was kind to me. I remained in that condition until a time when the Most High put all my dear ones in the like of that station. Then I saw Shaykh Abu ʿAbd Allah ibn Khafif, Shaykh Abu Ishaq Shahryar, Junayd, Ruwaym, Bayazid al-Bistami, and all the masters go on horseback together to the Transcendent One (glory be to him). They were standing before God, and Junayd and Abu Yazid had mercy on me. Several great masters wished to come nearer to the Truth (glory be to him) than I was. They all longed for him, and they shouted, danced, and shook, so that the world trembled from them.

✿ 162. Roses on the Mountain

I saw the Truth (glory be to him) on a holy mountain, and he made me approach. The mountain was high, and the Truth had me sit near him, and repeatedly gave me to drink of the wines of intimacy. He graced me in a form that I cannot tell to any of God's creatures. He was unveiled, and the lights of his beautiful attributes appeared from him. The Sufis were on the foothill of that mountain, unable to ascend the mountain. The Truth (glory be to him) called that mountain Mount Greatness. The lights of the world of oneness were joined to that mountain. I was intoxicated there, in such a state that the people of the world would if they saw me melt from my extreme beauty. God most high clothed me with the sublimities of his nature, and he scattered red roses that fell from my face and tresses. One rose fell from my face in the midst of the Sufis, and they shouted at that and began to dance.

Time passed, and my heart did not rest, from expansiveness, intimacy, and witnessing. God (glory be to him) drew me from Mount Greatness to the world of holiness, transcendence, eternity, pre-eternity, and post-eternity. Lights, sublimities, majesty, and beauty appeared to me, and the distance from the throne to the earth, next to that world, was smaller than an atom. I remained witnessing the Truth in the form of holiness for a time, and was there among the ecstatics, lovers, annihilated ones, transformed ones, knowers of God, the ignorant, and the learned. I longed to remain in that station because there is pure insight and the vision of vision. Then his luminosity seized me, and it hid me from him, and God most high nourished me. May your witnessing of him continue in that world!

⊛ 163. The Voices of Thunder

I sat at dawn seeking the witnessing of the hidden. I saw myself suddenly in a wide desert between mountains. Between me and the presence were heavy veils, and I heard the word of the Truth (glory be to him) speaking from beyond these veils. It was as though I heard great peals of thunder, and great thunderbolts in this likeness. Creation and time were melting with awe of his word. I did not comprehend what I heard from him, and I asked the Truth (glory be to him) if he would tell me what he was saying. He said, "I am saying, 'But his command, when he wishes a thing, is only that he says to it "Be!" and it is. Glory be to the one in whose hand is dominion over everything, and to him you shall return'" [Qurʾan 36:82]. I said to myself, "Creatures flee from the assault of his word; who can stand face to face with his power?" He unveiled his majesty and kept that veil uncovered for a time. I saw the Most High in the form of majesty and beauty, of awe and greatness. He drew me near to him, and strengthened me so that I saw him as I wished to. I saw all the prophets going mad in the deserts of the hidden, tyrannical, intoxicated, wounded, dyed with their own blood, which was shed in the assault of his majesty and the assaults of his greatness. Then I saw him nearer than that, having manifested himself to me all his attributes of loveliness and beauty in the station of expansiveness. He became expansive with me and said, "In this form in which you see me I went from the world of eternity to your town and your neighborhood before you were created, for your sake, seventy thousand times." During that time I was in the form of those who are drunk from happiness, agitation, applause, sighs, and tears. Time passed, and I was between sobriety and intoxication, presence and absence, annihilation and divine presence. I never heard anything from the Truth in my entire life like what I heard in these great voices.

❀ 164. From Striving to Grace

I recalled the days of discipleship, and the requirements of striving that had overwhelmed me, and their falling away from my heart over a space of twenty years. I remained without discipline or striving, and the chants of the masters and their many preceding disciplinary exercises fell away from my heart, as though I no longer approved of them in the court of knowledge. For knowledge with me makes use of grace and other things besides discipline and striving, otherwise it is the knowledge of the common people. I rejected such thought, and was concerned whenever a thought occurred to my heart. A visitation of the hidden befell me and the Truth (glory be to him) was unveiled to me twice, once in the form of beauty, and once in the form of greatness. I looked at the beauty of his transcendent face with the eye of the heart, and he said to me, "How can they reach me by strivings and disciplines, if my noble face remains veiled to them? This is reserved for my lovers and the near ones among the knowers of God; there is no way to me except through me, and by the unveiling of my beauty." After the ecstasies, the spiritual states, and the visitation, I returned to the creed of oneness and the election of his favor through what he wishes, to whom he wishes, as he wishes: "Grace is in the hands of God, he gives it to whom he wills" [Qurʾan 57:29]. And the sweetness of that remained until I slept.

❁ 165. Release from Fear

When I awakened, a fear of separation fell upon my heart, and I remembered days past and bygone sins. My fear increased, and I abased myself, saying, "My God! I fear your wrath on the Day of Resurrection, when my sins will be exposed before the knowers of God!" I saw myself in that hour above the utmost ʿIlliyyin in the presence of might, between the prophets and the sincere ones and the nearest angels, in the form of raving and rapture. I heard from beyond a veil something that quiets my heart from that, and all the sorrows fell away from me when I saw myself in the station of expansiveness. I was in the oceans of testing, and the vicissitudes of time befell me. I asked God most high for salvation from them, and said, "If you gave everything from the throne to the earth to a tiny ant, your kingdom would not be diminished by an atom, for in your hand are the keys to the fates of the nonexistent. In less than an instant, seventy thousand worlds issue from nonbeing by your encompassing power, from the worlds of kingdom and witnessing. What is this distress, and what is your opinion, master of those who would know God? Pacify me and purify me of all ambitions for anything but you. You gave the kingdom of Solomon to Solomon, and you gave the kingdom of David to David, and you gave the kingdom of Egypt to Joseph, though you had no obligation to them, Holy One." I was in that momentary state with prolonged sorrow and painful concern, but I endured a while.

❀ 166. The Garment of God

I saw the Truth (glory be to him) suddenly in the cracks in the hidden world, in the form of majesty and beauty, and he drew me near so that nothing remained between us; there was no between. Over and over he was kind to me, and made me see him as though he (who is transcendent and sanctified beyond change) wondered at my concerns. That is, it is not appropriate [to suppose that] his thinking should become confused like yours at the occurrence of suffering. During that time I was between intoxication and sobriety, and sighs and tears. Then he hid from me, then I saw him in that form and nearness. I saw him in the form of Adam facing the world of eternity, and he was in the form of greatness and beauty. The highlands of pre-eternity passed in front of me, and he looked at me with the eye of perfection, and magnified me, and left me in my form. I returned from the fields of oneness to the space of servanthood, raving and bewildered. The beauty of post-eternity was opened to me from the world of holiness, and he ravished me, and I was like a raving drunkard. The Truth (glory be to him) illuminated me with the light of the beauty of pre-eternity, and with it he filled creation and time. A light crossed the regions of the heavens and earth and shone upon his likeness, "for his is the highest likeness" [Qur'an 30:27], like the radiance of the red rose and red gold in a crucible. It overwhelmed everything. I said, "What is this?" It was said to me, "This is the manifestation of the garment of God." Then he cast into my mind his transcendent saying "We shall show them our signs on the horizons and in themselves," up to his saying "truly he witnesses everything" [Qur'an 41:53].

❀ 167. The Face in the Window

Then he hid, and then his face appeared from the window of the angelic realm, and he plundered my heart and spirit. Then his essence and attributes appeared, and he drew me near until there was only a cubit between us. I looked at his majesty and beauty, and I was intimate with him, and passionate, and I remained in that state for hours. Were it not for the grace and mercy of God when he appeared in the form of majesty, he would have consumed me with the flame of greatness and the lights of his sanctified sublimities. My heart flew in the form of longing in the air of 'Illiyyin, and the risings of the dawn of witnessing suddenly burst forth. All the prophets laughed at its light, and I saw myself in the desert of the hidden in the form of isolation. I heard the voice of God (glory be to him) from beyond the veils of greatness, and he said, "Welcome." I smiled and marveled and was happy and entered ecstasy, and my conscience and spirit were glad. Then the beauty of the Truth arose in the form of majesty and greatness. Everything became beautified by his beauty, and illuminated by his light, but between us were fields and wastelands. He was manifesting himself from one world into the temporal world. I remained in the enjoyment of intimacy and the sweetness of witnessing.

❀ 168. The Family in Paradise

Last night it was as though I saw myself in the desert of China, and the Truth (glory be to him) arose arrayed in the form of divinity, in the forms of Turks. He contacted me every instant with an unveiling in that station, and from witnessing him in my heart I found the delight of union and the attainment of beauty. Within an hour I saw him in this aspect seven times—God transcends the character of time, for he partakes of the character of holiness, transcendence, and freedom from all that is not appropriate to his power. I thought in my heart, recalling making a living, and remembering certain pieces of land, how they would turn out after me. The garden was unveiled to me, and I saw its rivers, trees, and castles. I saw my wife wearing the clothing of the people of paradise, and she was in the same form as they were; she was waiting at the door of one of the castles, as though she were expecting my arrival, and my delay in the world was to her but a moment. I saw a group of my wives, sons, daughters, and relatives, and I entered ecstasy, and my heart was happy to see them.

✦ 169. The Eye of Vision

Then I saw the world of ʿIlliyyin, and the veils of the presence were unveiled. I saw beyond a blue mountain the beauty of the sites where the Truth is witnessed, as though he had seized everything from Mount Qaf to Mount Qaf. I remained astonished and intimate with his majesty and beauty. That ended, night came, and was mostly gone. I saw the radiances of unveiling from the worlds of the hidden, but I was not satisfied with that. So he brought near to me that light and glory, and the Truth (glory be to him) appeared and sat by me (his greatness is transcendent), turning his face in the directions of his power, away from the witnessing of time. He said, "Look at me with the eye of vision." My heart, spirit, soul, intellect, and form were in the lights of his majesty, drowned in the oceans of intimacy and ecstasy. When my conscience was calm, I said, "My God! Become my hearing, sight, tongue, heart, spirit, intellect, and all my parts, and drown me in the oceans of your divinity, so I can look upon your essence and your attributes without a veil, forever, with passion, longing, love, and knowledge." Refreshing streams of ecstasy and flashes of manifestation descended upon my heart from the horizons of eternity, and I swam in the oceans of thought and remembrance. The nets of concentration were flung over the deserts of the hidden to trap the birds of the lights of might and the angelic realm. I saw in the beginnings of unveiling in my heart the joys of union.

✵ 170. The Attack of Crashing Oceans

Then the Truth (glory be to him) was unveiled to me on the highlands of eternity, in the wilderness of pre-eternity, so my inner consciousness was agitated, and I had no peace. The magnet of oneness attracted a heart of living steel to the station of nearness. So I fled to the Truth in the form of longing and eagerness, and my momentary state was that of disturbance and intimacy, of loss and ecstasy, and veiling and manifestation. The suns of the dawns of power passed to the sunsets of the hidden, and longing and intimacy were bequeathed to me. Disastrous states and visitations of the hidden descended upon me, and the crashing oceans of the lights of the attributes attacked me. The ocean of all time plunged me into its depth. I saw myself once in the air of all time, once in the deserts of eternity, and once in the oceans of post-eternity. The Truth (glory be to him) appeared to me in every state in the one of his attributes that he concealed from the eyes of creatures, which clothes the loveliness of the essence with a strange beauty and a strange majesty in a strange state. Here the knowers of God love him, and those with longing rave for him, and those who proclaim one God vanish beneath his authority.

✵ 171. The Attack of the Saints

I saw myself as though I were in the oases of spiritual states, in the midst of a desert. There the masters stood with their jeweled crowns and their couches, and in the hand of each was a frying pan, with which they threw stones at me continuously, as though throwing stones from a catapult. Our master and leader Abu Yazid (may God sanctify his spirit) was the most active in inciting this. But my state at that moment suffered there, and I sought God's help. The Truth (glory be to him) appeared and cast great stones at them, and they all settled down and threw away their frying pans. They approached me and were kind to me, and at that moment I reached the pavilions of greatness. I saw all the prophets, messengers, angels, and saints. The one most ancient in the Truth, in presence, and the closest of them to God most high was our Prophet. Then came the senior prophets, such as Adam, Idris, Noah, Abraham, Moses, and their equals among the prophets. And they pushed me, as though they wished to overwhelm me. The transcendent Truth approached me from the left, and he was like a column of red gold. He turned to me and his face was light. The Truth (glory be to him) manifested himself, and God most high honored me there. When they saw me in the form in which God the transcendent had clothed me, by the doors of power, every prophet and sincere one took his drink from the wine of the presence, showing me which of them would drink for me and for the love of me. Then I saw the Truth (glory be to him) with his drink, and he showed them that he took it for my sake and for love of me, and this was the perfection of his grace to the servant of the Most High. I awoke in the night with delight and happiness, singing free, un-willed sounds like the buzzing of bees.

✸ 172. Hide and Seek

I performed ablutions and prayed two cycles, and ecstasy overcame me during prayer. When I prayed, God spoke to me with noble invocations and gracious remembrances in my free prayer. He opened for my heart the doors of free prayer. What was in my heart came easily to my tongue, and the secrets of oneness and the graces of expansiveness were expressed on my tongue. The clouds of the hidden rained upon my conscience the rain of realities and subtleties. I spoke with the tongue of the prophets, and then I asked him for the vision of knowledge and perception. My concentration did not rise beyond existence; I did not know that he was with me.

He appeared to me and said, "Where are you, when I am with you?" Then he hid, and then he surprised me; he seized me and tumbled me through the heavens of substantiality and the pavilions of majesty. I saw him in the abode of majesty in "the most beautiful form"; if the cherubs saw him in that form, they would all melt from the effect of his loveliness and his beauty. Then he made me enter the world of the sublimities of the essence, and between us were sublimities and oceans of holiness, shining more than the atoms of being. These were veils closer than which I could not approach by so much as the head of a pin. Here creation and time threw me, and I was astonished in the heart of my understanding at the form of the Truth (glory be to his majesty). I returned as one bewildered and lost. I was in the best of the brief states that arise from purity, and here was nothing but pure remembrance of God's names, without disturbance. Union dawned suddenly, and the armies of manifestation passed the beauty of the Truth. I saw him as though he sought to manifest himself to increase my longing for him. Then I sought him after midnight, and I said to myself, "Would that I had seen the Truth (glory be to him) in the form of eternity!" Then he appeared to me in the most beautiful shape. He said, facing me, "Do you doubt that I am the lord of the worlds?"

✿ 173. The Stilling of the Rain

Then I saw above the throne in the bridal canopies of intimacy, that he manifested himself in the form of majesty and beauty. There was no one in front of the Truth except Gabriel, who was weeping, having torn his clothes for the sake of the beauty of the Truth that had overwhelmed him. Then that time passed, and I was concerned about whether the rain and snow would continue. But the sublimities in the sky were not unveiled. I saw a desert in which a great river flowed like pearls. I saw Khidr and Ilyas (peace be upon them) with all the Substitutes there, washing their clothes.

I saw nothing better than the vision of them at that time. I thought that this was the stilling of the rain, but God knows best.

❀ 174. Showers of Jewels

It happened one night that I was distressed on account of a quarrel with my family, and their complaint about certain necessities. I awoke after midnight, and I despaired about the openings of the hidden. My conscience settled, my intimacy continued, and my spirit was graced. I awaited the wonders of unveiling of the world on the angelic realm, and I saw the Truth (glory be to him) arrayed in the form of divinity, in an assembly. My momentary state was joyful, my conscience was agitated, my longing increased, and my ecstasy multiplied. I was disturbed and shouted. Then he hid from me, and opened the world of the angelic realm. I saw oceans of new pearls, and he (glory be to him) seized gems from them and showered them over my head repeatedly. So also did the prophets and the angels, until I reached the world of eternity. The Truth (glory be to his majesty) manifested himself in the form of pre-eternity, and there was the place of annihilation. Then he hid from me and I fell into the state of dust, "where the fruits of every thing are brought as sustenance from us" [Qur'an 28:57]. Then he said to me, "Is it not true that I am, from above the throne to the stable earth, the ruler of creatures and that the keys of everything are in my hand? I administer my kingdom as I have shown you. Does not the flow of fates issue from my will? Say, they are meddlers and people who complain about me; they must stop their complaint and give thanks to me for the equivalence of my bounty—otherwise I will destroy them." I was made afraid by this rebuke, for by it he had demonstrated his dominion. I awoke in the night after midnight, near dawn, and my sleep had been a sweet sleep.

❈ 175. Gazing at Beauty

I sat for meditation, and I saw on the bench of my house the Truth (glory be to him) unveiled of the robes of power, pure and dressed in majesty and beauty. He was acting as a beloved does with a lover, scattering from the beauty of his transcendent face a loveliness that, if Mount Qaf looked at it and saw the Most High in that form, it would melt from the sweetness of his beauty and the loveliness of union with him. I remained in that for hours, and sighs and tears overpowered me. Then he unveiled to me the world of holiness, and I saw him in the world of the angelic realm, and in the world of majesty in the form of beauty. He manifested himself from his beauty as that world, and I saw all that I had seen in the form of the beauty of the Truth. I saw none of the prophets, saints, and highest angels except with that beauty. I saw our Prophet, and he was drowned in that form, qualified by this attribute, and he was dancing. So also were all the prophets and angels. He brought me still nearer, and I saw him as though I saw the likeness of the full moon, with planets around it. It was a garment for beggars in the station of being clothed with divinity. The moon was the Truth (glory be to him), and these planets were the angels. The nearest of them to the Most High was Gabriel. It was as though they never hoped for anything from him, and as though they loved him passionately. The Most High was kind to them as though they were his family. Then he brought me near, and increased my nearness from the world of substance and eternity. I halted before his power and gazed upon him for hours. The doors of angels were closed to me, and these stations were bequeathed to me in intimacy, passion, love, and eloquence. Then God most high made peace descend on my heart, from which all worldly sorrows departed. May God increase us and you in the loveliness of his nearness and the nobility of his nearness.

❀ 176. The Turk with the Lute

I passed to the dawn of eternity, and I saw in the desert of the hidden that the Truth (glory be to him) arose in the form of beauty in the shape of Turks. In his hand was a lute, and he acted like he was playing that lute. It agitated me, increasing my passion and longing. I became restless from the ecstatic pleasure of beauty and the loveliness of union. Then I saw him in the world of eternity, passing to the world of post-eternity. There was no place, dimension, light, shadow, disposition, or form there, but it was illuminated by the manifestation of God. He found me a stranger there, and the lights of his qualities brought me near, and he drowned me in the oceans of the sublimities of his essence. Then I saw him, and I was in my room, as though he were visiting me. He was of a beauty and a loveliness that I cannot describe. I wept for him and implored him, saying, "My God! Keep me gazing at you for an hour, and drive out of my heart all that is not you, from the throne to the earth. You are the beloved of the hearts of the knowers of God, and the delight of the mad lovers!" So he stayed a while.

❀ 177. Unveiled in actions

Then I saw him at the door of my friends' house, calling them and saying to them, "People of my fortress," meaning "Arise in obedience to me." But the moment passed, and it lessened my intoxication. The time of invocations was gone, and I recalled the realities of oneness and the stages of ecstasies. I said to myself, "What are these cloaks of the forms of divinity, which have plundered me of the graces of those who are alone with him? What veil separates me from union with the realities?" The source of the attributes was unveiled to me in actions. My head moved and turned without my willing it, and my vision plunged me into the oceans of ecstasy and spiritual states; those who make the effort [in meditative exercises] can act this way at will. I said, "Soul, how can my head move, if the transcendent Truth is not unveiled to me in the clothing of actions? Do not be concerned about me taking steps in the test of love." Everything is drowned in the manifestation of the Truth, who appears in everything to the eyes of inner consciousness.

✿ 178. Deserts of Eternity and Taverns of Union

When an hour passed, I saw myself in the deserts of eternity, and I saw the Truth (glory be to him) on the streets and paths of pre-eternity, facing post-eternities. I joined him in that journey. He made me see him as though he had traveled to me from the wombs of the eternity of eternities. Distance there is not limited, because a step in the likeness of that road is farther than from the throne to the steady earths. When I traveled with him, I said, "My God! (And he was in the form of majesty and beauty.) How can I cross the distance of post-eternities with you? I want to look at you for an hour." He stopped for me, and I gazed upon his majesty and the beauty of his transcendent face. I was enraptured and enamored. Then I saw myself beneath the pavilions of the kingdom in the world of might, drowned in the ocean of blood, and that blood was from my eye. I was sunk in that ocean for long hours. The transcendent Truth seized me, and I was in a state of raving. He seated me on the carpet of his nearness, and he gave me to drink of the wine of brilliance. Then I saw him in the abode of majesty, then I saw him in the taverns of union, with my boon companions, knowers of God. Then he took me and stood me before him, and he manifested sublimities and those sublimities struck the world. The world reeled from those assaults, since existing beings and time vanished from his power and the appearance of his greatness.

❀ 179. The "Praiseworthy Station" and Abandonment

Then I saw all the prophets, sincere ones, and the nearest angels in the presence of God most high, in rapture and agitation. The Transcendent One manifested himself to them, and then they were all veiled from the Truth, except for Muhammad. He was in a form of loveliness and beauty, halting by the door to the abode of majesty like the chamberlain with the emperor. He was looking at the Truth and speaking with the Truth, and no one was with him in that station. I knew that this was the "praiseworthy station" [Qur'an 17:79]. But I saw the Most High afterward in the gaps in those veils. Then the transcendent Truth manifested himself to me in the form of oneness and seized me with his powerful hand. He took me to the world of eternity, where I was senseless and over-powered, until he made me enter primordial journeys. I saw oceans upon oceans, greatness upon greatness, fields upon fields, and I nearly was annihilated in the accumulated oceans of pre-eternity. When he realized my inability to bear the weight of the anguish of oneness, he abandoned me and left. I returned to where I was.

❀ 180. Beyond Imagination

One night I was confronted with psychic imaginings, trivial imaginings, and spiritual imaginings. I tore their veils and saw their graces, and I thought about some of their shapes, from the sight of which my heart had fled. I was distressed by the sight of some of them, and I was astonished at my rank, until the beauty of God appeared to me suddenly, and there was such loveliness and beauty that I cannot describe it. I said, "My God! What are these likeness-es in which I have been veiled before witnessing?" He said, "This is for one who seeks me in the first unveilings of my majesty, until he knows me through these veils, and this is the station of knowledge;

one who only knows me through them is not a [true] knower of me. This is the station of striving for the people of witnessing." Then he made me enter the veils of the hidden, and showed me his attributes with most of the clothing of majesty and beauty. Then he hid, and I abased myself before him, because I had found the sweetness of union and the pleasure of longing for beauty.

✸ 181. The Attack of the Lion, and a Funeral

Then I saw the Most High in the form of pre-eternity, having already manifested himself from the world of the hidden. I saw Khidr, Ilyas, all the leaders of the Substitutes, and the masters. There were hospices under their protection, as there are for Sufi travelers. They placed these hospices in the utter deserts of the hidden. They cast themselves in these deserts before God. Then I saw the Prophet with all the [other] prophets and messengers and angels, doing as the Substitutes and masters had done. They were rolling in those deserts before the might of God most high. I was standing there weeping at God, by God, for God. Then his power fell upon me. I saw existence annihilated by the assaults of his power, and I saw in those deserts that a lion emerged, which I cannot describe. It was clothed in the greatness of God, and all the prophets, saints, and angels fled from it, but I was standing there. It attacked me once; it leapt upon me; then it let me go, though it stayed there for a while. Then God isolated me in an assembly in the abode of intimacy, and this was in the form of beauty, but no other of his creatures was there. It was as though God elected me for union, and I was in the condition of intoxication from overwhelming bewilderment.

I thought in my heart about my death in the middle of some night. My heart was happy at the light that befell it, and my limbs opened up, and my hair and skin were luminous. I saw the people of the angelic realm turning their beautiful faces to me, wearing the clothes of condolence, in a form more beautiful than I had ever seen. Then I saw Gabriel, Michael, Israfil, and ʿAzraʾil, the bearers of the throne, and all the angels, all wearing hats on their heads of frightening aspect. So also was our Prophet, and all the prophets and saints. I saw the Truth (glory be to him) manifest himself to me arrayed in the form of divinity, and he appeared to me as though he were giving condolences. Then he came to me, and with him were all the prophets, messengers, angels, and saints, and he took me by the hand and brought me to the world of majesty and beauty, in a presence, with gardens, and happiness. Then the houris removed the veils from their heads, and passed cups around, in which was wine, and the angels sang. The Truth (glory be to him) said to me, "This is how your death will be."

❀ 182. Unveilings of Form

Once during a time of weakness, when I was distressed, I saw that the Truth (glory be to him) was standing in the deserts of the angelic realm in the world of eternity, facing me after unveiling his beauty, as though he made me see the qualities of his existence. He bequeathed that until the time of morning, in happiness and sweet moments. Gardens of roses were unveiled, but I was far from witnessing God. He manifested himself to me from the branches of the red rose, and he had red roses with him, which he gave to me. He taught me that unveilings do not manifest themselves except by the will of God and pre-eternal election. He cheered me with the manifestation of the qualities of attributes, he perfumed my heart with the knowledge that he is mine, and he achieves this for no cause. Then he showed me his beauty, dressed in the clothing of power and grandeur and greatness, until he showed me the eye of eternity arrayed in the form of divinity, and the form of pre-eternality. I was in the time of passion and the flow of his commands in the pleasure of spiritual witnessing. I was freed from having God most high show me the shapes of the angelic realm in the form of man, from my excessive love for beautiful faces. He showed me much of his transcendent beauty in the form that the Prophet mentioned in his saying, "I saw my lord in the most beautiful form."

❁ 183. The Banishment of Satan

The accursed Satan knew of my condition, and he dived into the ocean of his deception. He presented me with satanic imaginings and psychic likenesses. I recognized them all, but how did my thought insinuate that what I saw of the world of the angelic realm and the attributes of the transcendent Truth came from his miserable semblances and likeness? My conscience feared and my heart was averse to that thought, and I was distressed when words fell between him and Moses: "The one who speaks to you is not God most high." And Moses ceased speaking until God purified him of his evil by revealing miracles. Beyond that, God made me look differently on the thoughts that occurred to me, saying, "How can there be sighs, sobs, tears, the preparation of consciences with the occurring of lights, and the increase of longing for witnessing eternity, on account of the likeness of Satan? Do not be concerned. I am I, the one who chooses to manifest himself to the pure in the form that pleases their hearts. There is no genuine ecstasy except from the manifestation of my witnessing, in whatever state it may be. I am the one who manifests himself. When manifestation occurs to them, their hearts are looted, and their spirits fly in the world of the angelic realm and might. They know how to sanctify me and declare my transcendence of relationships with semblances, peers, or opposites. Do not fear or sorrow; I congratulate you, for you are one of the emperors of my saints and one of those elected for my love and knowledge."

⚘ 184. From the
Dawning Orient

I was in the station of confidences, tales, and secrets unfolded. The Truth (glory be to him) showed me kindness by unveiling his lights, and the north wind of union blew in the deserts of my heart. My heart was assailed by the glory of the lightning of his holiness and the radiance of his majesty. He appeared to me and took from me every station and statement. He bequeathed to me a sweetness of heart, refreshment of spirit, agitation of conscience, and forgetfulness of all else. He drowned me in the ocean of ecstasy and spiritual states, and made sighs, rapture, tears, and sobs appear from me. When that station was perfected, the Truth (glory be to him) dawned upon me from the East of the hidden in a form that—My brother! I want you to see him in that form, and by God! If Mount Qaf saw him in that state, it would melt from the sweetness of witnessing him. It was as though he arose from the world of roses, glory, light, and lights. My conscience was reckless and my intellect was baffled, my heart was annihilated, and my eyes stared. I was in such a state, that if one of the angels that are nearest to God, or a prophetic messenger had seen me, they would have envied me.

⚘ 185. Encounter with
Revelation

Then that passed, and after midnight I was in a station where the breezes of power scatter. The Truth (glory be to him) manifested himself to me in the condition of beauty. He increased my passion and longing, he agitated me so that I would compose poetry, and applaud, and weep, and he passed time with me. May God endow us and you with abundant great miracles and exemplary gifts! The source of this unveiling is the encounter with special revelation, after I awoke but before I arose from my bed. He said, "I endowed you with a love from me, so that you would be nourished in my sight" [Qur'an 20:39]. I knew that he would come with gifts of secrets and sparks of light. There remained in my heart the memory of certain stations in witnessings that were disclosed to me on certain nights. The ache they produced lingered in my head, recalling these sanctified virtues. Ecstasies and visitations prevented me from remembering them. When I entered the oceans of pure remembrance of God's names, the Truth (glory be to him) unveiled himself to me in the form of beauty and majesty, from the direction of the north pole. He said to me, "My servant, to me, to me!" This gladdened my heart with a sweetness that would have made reckless the intellects of any people of the earth who tasted it, and would have made their hearts fly away.

❀ 186. Beyond the Veils of Eternity

I saw the Most High also in the form of beauty from the direction of the east, until my heart arrived at a station where it saw him manifesting himself with rose-colored clothing and red light. With him was a mirage, by which he made me see as though he had brought me there for myself. Then he hid from me, and I entered the oceans of the hidden until I reached the veils of eternity. The Most High manifested himself in the form of eternity, and he made me stop. I saw all creation and time smaller than a mustard seed in a field. After that, I found no way to the world of eternity, and I could not look at the wombs of pre-eternity. No, here, the oceans of primordiality surged, and there was no place one could see in it. God transcends what runs in the thoughts of those who reduce him to abstraction and the fancies of those who understand God in human terms. I was among the witnesses of spiritual imaginings, and I saw among the armies traces of the lights of the Truth on the essences of the special attributes in actions. When the vision of these attributes passed, the Truth manifested to me the virtues of eternity, but he manifested them in the form of the special beauty that is cloaked with divinity over the attribute of the source of the essence. I gazed at the graces of the attributes in their different clothes, until he made me enter the veils of the bridal canopies of majesty and holiness. I saw veils of the red rose that the Truth (glory be to him) beautified with the light of his glory. The Most High was unveiled among the veils in the world of sanctity, and I saw a multitude beyond every veil, fallen down before me. The Truth (glory be to him) said, "Beyond every veil, a hundred Gabriels are killed with the sword of longing." Then he seized me and made me enter the world of power and divine presence and eternity. I saw the Most High in the form of primordiality that frightens away with its attacks both spirits and intellects. My brother! I fell in stations of the witnesses of majesty; I would like to describe them to people so that they would love him passionately, and be annihilated in the sublimities of his greatness. This is from my love for him, my mercy for his servants, and my sorrow for them; how can they be cut off from him, with nothing?

❀ 187. Mountains of Sugar

I prostrated to God in a state of freeing my night journey from the crowding of dangerous insinuations and the turmoil of reprehensible thoughts. I saw one of my wives who had died in my presence, and in her hand was a piece of white sugar. She placed it in my mouth, and then I saw her in the midst of mountains of sugar; it was a world of white sugar shining with light. I saw my father, mother, children, and grandchildren in that world, and they were gladdened by me. Then I saw the Truth (glory be to him) manifest himself from the hidden beyond that world, and he suddenly passed by me. Then thoughts of him testing me occurred to my conscience, and the Truth (glory be to him) called out to me [the words he addressed to the Prophet], "By the pen, and that which they write, you are not, by your lord's favor, a madman, and yours shall be a limitless reward; you are of great character" [Qurʾan 68:1–4]. My thoughts departed by the grace of God most high. Then he manifested himself to me from the world of spring and roses, in the form of majesty and beauty. He was in a form such as you would have seen me, as the companion of the presence, the chief of the angelic realm, the lover of the age, and the warrior of the field of love. "It is the kindled fire of God that consumes up to the hearts" [Qurʾan 104:6–7]. I did not know what this burning was.

❁ 188. Patched Sufi Cloaks

The Truth manifested himself from the world of greatness and oneness, and he clothed me with his light and his glory. I remained witnessing him for a long time, and I heard different kinds of utterance. Then that ascension and path passed away, and I heard a crier say, "The sanctified ones come." I saw the great masters, Junayd, Ruwaym, Sari, Maʿruf, Abu Yazid al-Bistami, Dhu al-Nun al-Misri, our master Abu ʿAbd Allah ibn Khafif, our master Abu al-Hasan ibn Hind, and all the other Sufi masters. Then I saw all the companions [of the Prophet], and all of them were wearing patched clothing. They were dancing and entering ecstasy. In the hands of one great one was a drum, and he played the drum and wore a patched cloak. Then they gathered before the Prophet. He had arisen from his grave, and his face was like a red rose. His tresses were like pungent musk, and he wore a patched cloak. Thus I saw all the prophets, the first of them Adam, and the last of them Muhammad. I saw Gabriel with the great angels, and they wore patched cloaks. The Prophet preceded all creatures before God (glory be to him), and the Truth (glory be to him) appeared to us. I was among them like a drunken companion, with a lute in my hand, singing and playing. God most high chose me for nearness, from among all creatures, and he spoke to me of marvelous secrets and extraordinary news. Praise be to God, who supplies his bounties and is more than sufficient. I was distressed by the lights of testing, the tension of the radiances of witnessing, and the accumulation of weakness. My heart was fleeing from God; it sought to hide in the valley of natural darknesses and to emerge from the station of meditation and study of the world of eternity into the stations of desires and accidents. This distress was due to the wrath of his jealousy, when he tested his servants who are affected by the calamities of the veil.

✸ 189. The Abode of Majesty

I was sitting one night, and I spoke of my importance and my rank, so that I became stronger in the world of imaginings and familiar with satanic likenesses. My conscience reached the margins of the world of wrathful actions; it did not turn toward the presence, and it did not look upon the places where manifestation falls. It lowered its eyes from the witnessing of the hidden lights, and hours passed in that. I saw the abode of majesty suddenly, and God (glory be to him) manifested himself to me arrayed in the form of divinity. I was overwhelmed by that which overwhelmed the ecstatics during their witnessing of majesty, with sighs, tears, rapture, and bewilderment. He manifested himself to me on another occasion. The abode of majesty was filled with the Truth (glory be to him), and my conscience, heart, intellect, spirit, exterior, and interior were happy. I was full of gladness, wakefulness, intimacy, happiness. Every veil and every reproach left my thoughts behind. I remained hopeful of further stations and a happiness that sweetens union. Then I was gladdened by the wayfaring of servanthood, and by bearing weights in hope of lordship.

❈ 190. Journeys of the Heart

I sent my heart to the world of time, and it reached the earth. Then it turned from the lower angelic realm to the higher angelic realm, and it turned above the throne; nothing existent remained with it. Then it crossed the wasteland of eternity between time and eternity. It reached the witnesses of lordship by way of the unveiling of the radiances of special actions to which existence is connected. Then it shot into the station of astonishment at lordship, the vision of the lights of action, the effects of power, and the wrath of eternity. Then the greatness of God most high and his majesty appeared to it, and it was as though it were in between the layers of surging oceans. Then it saw the infinitely great one, who is the form of the eternal essence. It was annihilated in the vision of the essence, and it acquired no comprehension or knowledge. But the Most High made it see him without obscurity, and it remained there for hours, seeking the bestowal of rapture, bewilderment, sighing, and tears from that station. Then it resumed the journeys of eternity and saw the Truth (glory be to him) in the form of beauty, and he was facing it as though he appeared from the world of roses and light. He was kind to it with rare kindness. Then God most high appeared to it from another world, from the worlds of red roses, where the chosen presence was. God most high saw it, and God seized it by the hand, and embraced it and called out in the worlds of holiness, "This is a king. 'Whose is the kingdom?'" [Qurʾan 40:16] From that station appeared chosen passion, chosen love, intimacy, and divine presence.

❈ 191. The Omnipresent Beauty

Then the beauty of the Most High appeared to me in different kinds of people, all being kind to me because of the divine presence in me after my annihilation in the qualities of pre-eternity. He gave me to drink of the wine of intimacy and nearness. Then he left, and I saw him as the mirror of creation wherever I faced, as he says, "Wheresoever you turn, there is the face of God" [Qurʾan 2:115]. Then he spoke to me after increasing my longing for him, and that was after I had a thought, and said to myself, "I want to see his beauty without interruption." He said, "Remember the condition of Zulaykha and Joseph, for Zulaykha depicted her form to Joseph in all six directions, so that Joseph did not see in any direction without seeing her form there. This is your condition in the abode of my majesty." I saw God from every atom, though he transcends incarnation and human forms. But he is a secret known only to those drowned in the oceans of oneness and to the knower of the secret of the actions of eternity in the station of passionate love.

❀ 192. In the Sight of God

When I stayed there long in bewilderment and agitation, my heart thought, "Take me from this strange land to my homeland." I wanted to know how my state would be. The Truth (glory be to him) appeared to me and spoke in my breast [something that] runs like the saying of the Most High [to Moses], "[I endowed you with a love from me] so that you would be nourished in my sight" [Qurʾan 20:39], and [concerning Noah's ark], "it sailed in our sight" [Qurʾan 54:14]. Then he said, "I am your bringer of good tidings." Then my heart thought, "How will my condition be here?" And all the people of that land abased themselves here before me, like sleepers fallen to the ground. God wanted by that means to show them to me and to teach me that they have no weight in my stations before him. His intention is that existence be empty; he is sufficient for me in all my goals.

✤ 193. Borne by Surging Oceans

Then he seized me with ecstasies, visitations, and overflowing secrets, until a time of wakefulness near midnight; this was one of my journeys. My friend, may God nourish you and us with abundant nearness and the grace of his secrets. When my heart approached the world of eternity, the miraculous actions of the Most High appeared in the angelic realm of greatness. Then the oceans of oneness appeared to me, and their waves bore me to the witnessing of greatness. I saw the beauty of eternity in a form, without asking how. All creation and time shrank before the majesty of his greatness, until no trace of them remained in the dawning of the power of the glory of pre-eternity. I was there in the place of nearness, but the surging oceans of divine presence seized me, and were it not for the generosity of the Truth (glory be to him) who grasped my soul during the assaults of greatness, they would have annihilated it in less than an instant. It was as though the Most High showed me the qualities of singleness, and it was as though he indicated to me that I should look at his great majesty and beauty. That was a grace from him, and I drew near. At that time I was in the condition of rapture and sighing. Then he suddenly appeared to me after the world of holiness passed by this state, as though he were a sailor [amid the] oceans.

✤ 194. Flight of the Falcon

I saw the Truth (glory be to him) without asking how. In the pavilions of his greatness were the chosen prophets and the angels, in the form of white falcons. Then I flew near to our lord (who is transcendent and sanctified), and it was as though I were on the right side of the throne. I was like a racer among the falcons, and I was like one filled with longing. I flew for a while, and roamed for a while, and sat for a while like one enraptured, disturbed. The

Truth (glory be to him) spoke to me as I neared him, saying in Persian, "As you were, so were you freed [*chun budi, chun rasti*]." Then that state passed, but I stayed there, and from happiness I nearly melted from pleasure and content. I asked to witness divinity arrayed in the form of beauty, until I asked to play a lute while in a state of intoxication, passion, and longing for him. I saw the Most High at the banks of the rivers of the gardens of paradise, wearing clothing of red roses, bending his transcendent face with satisfaction and acceptance. The commands of the armies of passion overwhelmed me there.

✾ 195. Facing God's Majesty for All Creation

Then I saw myself in a house filled with light, and beneath that house I saw a man, one of my companions who had died, as though he were begging. He was a man who claimed several stations, and he claimed love. The Truth (glory be to him) manifested himself to me from the light of his holiness with the appearance of the witnessing of his face, and I was there like a gnat flying against storm winds. Then I saw all of creation pass beneath that house, until the most terrible of beasts were there. It was as though they were in need of me and that station. There all the creatures ceased to dread the assault of God's transcendent majesty upon me.

✾ 196. Seeking the Seeker

Then he exposed me to the radiances of holiness and the lights of divine presence—glory be to him, for he transcends all that does not match his quality. My conscience agreed to seek the sublime and the splendid, starting from the world of the hidden, so I traversed time and reached the edge of eternity. I heard the word of the Truth (glory be to him) from the hiding place of pre-eternity, saying, "I created existence to seek me, and you have reached the station of holiness; who is there like you in the world? I seek you underneath my foot." He appeared to me in the form of divinity, holiness, and transcendence. Everything other than him from the throne to the earth vanished beneath the assaults of his greatness. I witnessed him with visual witnessing, and it was the witnessing of the eye of greatness. He appeared in the witnessing of the beauty of divine presence—and that is a strange thing, since he [usually] displays the manifestation of beauty in the form of greatness. He agitated my conscience, made my intellect nothing, and tore my heart to bits. I was there for some time. Then he said, "You are seeking me and I am seeking you; if you look, you will find me in yourself, without taking the journeys of the hidden."

❀ 197. Reciting the Names of God

Before this visitation I was concerned about some utterances of members of my assembly, when I heard some nonsense of sayings that understand God in human terms. I explained his transcendent speech, saying that his speech is eternal, and whatever is not his speech is temporal. The Most High said, "I have made my speech transcendent; do not fear, for I myself preside whenever your assembly recites [my names]." I saw him appear, with all the cherubs and spiritual beings with him in my assembly. I saw the dwellers in the chosen presence walk around my assembly, and I saw Gabriel, wearing the clothes of a youth, giving water to the people in the great mosque from a water skin around his neck. When the assembly grew, I saw all the mountains reciting [God's names]. I [could tell] the mountains from each other; some had taller peaks than others, like men. I saw the heavens come to my assembly in the form of people, and likewise the throne, the footstool, paradise, and hell, and all the spirits of the prophets, sincere ones, martyrs, houris, heavenly youths, and children, all joined in the presence of the transcendent Truth. Then the Truth (glory be to him) spoke: "Do thus whenever there is an assembly for reciting [my names]." At that time I was in oceans of ecstasies, sobbing, bewildered, and raving, until my conscience found peace and he closed the doors of the angelic realm. He transcends every fancy that is inappropriate to his majesty, and he is beyond the witnessing of time and relations with creatures.

❀ 198. Love beyond Sorrow

I watched God most high after midnight on Thursday night, and time passed. Nothing was opened to me, but after that he manifested himself to me in the form of majesty, beauty, eternal loveliness, and the glory of pre-eternity. He ravished me and sat me down like a lover, crying out and weeping, announcing his majesty and beauty. I saw him in one of the forms of his divine presence in the station of intimacy and holiness; if either the ancients or the moderns had seen him, they would have flown reckless and bewildered through wastelands and deserts. Their limbs and joints would have been torn apart, and their intellects would have vanished. May God increase his eternal favors to us through his grace and generosity. I sat down to behold the hidden, and my conscience departed to the border of time. I reached the fields of pre-eternity, and the Truth (glory be to him) welcomed me and said, "I have journeyed for your sake from the heart, from the valleys of identity; in each of its valleys existence is smaller than a mustard seed. My only goal is to visit you; sometimes I have helped you while you are sleeping, from the start of the evening to the time of awaking." Then he manifested himself with a thousand attributes in a thousand stations, each with the quality of annunciation and satisfaction. Whenever I saw him in an attribute, he said to me, "I love you. No sorrow will affect you, because [one only feels] it after a loss. I remain yours, so do not sorrow, nor be distressed because of thoughts and calamities." When I heard that, and I had said to him what I heard from him, I entered the oceans of ecstasies, and sobs and tears overwhelmed me. I forgot no more in this unveiling than I extolled.

❀ 199. Approval of the Imams, and the Prophet's Ascension

The doors of the angelic realm were opened to me, and I saw in the deserts of the hidden the great imams in a circle on a carpet of light. I saw al-Shafiʿi, Abu Hanifa, Malik, and Ahmad ibn Hanbal, wearing white clothes and white turbans, rejoicing and congratulating one another at [seeing] my face. Then I saw above them the prophets, and I saw our Prophet Muhammad among his companions, above all other creatures. He left them and overtook me, rejoicing and smiling, and he was kind to me, saying, "I saw the saints and masters, and I saw Gabriel and Michael, and the poles of the cherubs. Then I reached the greatest angelic realm and saw the throne and the footstool. I saw a world of white pearls, and the Truth (glory be to him) welcomed me in the form of majesty and beauty, facing me on the plain of the attributes, in the form of satisfaction. The veiled ones of majesty and beauty appeared, and he showered pearls and jewels from the lights of his power. I never saw anything whiter than those gems, from the throne to the earth."

❀ 200. The Doors of the Presence

It happened that I sat after midnight during the month of Rajab [August 1189], and I was concerned about the people, because of a severe widespread plague. I found an intimate friend in my thoughts, and I saw everyone in the shape of that intimate friend. That was in the time of the flight of the armies of wrath from existence, the appearance of the influences of God's transcendent generosity, and the loveliness of his favor. I sat for a while and wondered if I had a basis for desiring unveilings of the hidden and witnessings of the lord (glory be to him). The doors of the angelic realm were opened to me, some following upon the others. Then I saw the Truth (glory be to him) in the form of majesty and beauty, as he appeared from the first door. He said, "I opened for you seven thousand doors of the presence of my grandeur and my greatness." Then he made me enter the first door, and I stayed there one thousand years. Then he made me enter all the doors, and I stayed in each door one thousand years. When I departed from all the doors, I saw the Most High in a form different from his attributes. I saw him in every door in another form; if creation had seen him in that form, it would have died from the pleasure. I cannot describe what I have seen from him of majesty and beauty and glory and sublimities.

❀ 201. Prophets, Angels, and the Infinite Presence

Then I saw the chosen ones at the door of the presence. There in the field of pre-eternity was our Prophet Muhammad, coming from the right hand of the presence. He was like a white pearl, and he had on clothes of pearl. Likewise I saw Adam wearing clothes of pearl. The Prophet embraced me and kissed my face, and so did Adam. Adam was extremely kind to me, like a father with a son. Then I saw Abraham, Moses, Jesus, and the elect prophets. I went to the nearness of the presence and saw Gabriel in the form of the Turks. He was like a red rose, and so was Israfil, amidst the presence. I approached the nearness of the presence, and I saw the Truth (glory be to him), more beautiful than I had seen him. He manifested himself to me repeatedly, each time in a different form. I saw wonders of seclusion from him. When he manifested himself in the form of splendor and happiness, he was manifesting to me the qualities of the attributes, until he plundered my heart more than he had ever plundered it before in my entire life, with that seclusion and that unveiling and witnessing. Then the fields of glory, the sublimities of eternity, the lights of divine presence, and the oceans of greatness became clear to me. God hid after that in the veils of the hidden. I remained there in the form of astonishment with the pleasure of ecstasy, spiritual states, tears, and sighs, until I returned to the first state. This unveiling was one of the rarities of the unknown sciences; creatures do not know its realities because their sciences are incomplete and their intellects defective.

✸ 202. Plague and Remedy

It happened that I sat before midnight with my son Ahmad, when he had a severe fever. All my heart melted from concern. Suddenly I saw the Truth (glory be to him) in the form of majesty, and he was kind to me and to him, though he was sleeping. Ecstasy and agitation overwhelmed me, but my soul settled down from the disturbance, lest he should awaken. That was difficult for me. I said, "My God! Why do you test me, when I am waiting for your help?" He said, "Do not sorrow; I am yours." I said, "My God! Why do you not speak to me as you spoke to Moses?" He said, "Be satisfied that whoever loves you loves me, and whoever sees you sees me." When I heard that, many ecstasies overwhelmed me. I stood, and the Truth (glory be to him) called out to the wombs of the hidden and said, "Remedy!" And a remedy came to him. Now the town was filled with the sick, unlike anything we ever saw. But the cure was released to the town, and it spread throughout all of Fars. I was in ecstasy, spiritual states, and crying. He was kind to my son, and gave him to drink.

❀ 203. The Hierarchy of Saints

Then after that, I saw him repeatedly in different attributes, until I saw him in the attributes of majesty, beauty, divinity, divine presence, and eternity. Then the Truth (glory be to him) stood, and I saw all time from the throne to the earth, before him, like the smallest of things. Then he unveiled to me the garment of greatness. He hid from me, then after that I saw, after my rest from ecstasy, the seven saints in the air of desire. Then behind them came Khidr and the pole, and the pole was a knight on horseback, who went ahead. Then he turned to me, and he was like a red rose. I saluted them repeatedly, and my heart rejoiced at seeing them. I knew that they came to gladden my heart.

❀ 204. The Gardens of Pre-Eternity

It happened that I was sitting one Thursday in Shiraz in the month of Rajab after midnight, and in my inner consciousness I was navigating around the ocean of pre-eternity, for two purposes: to seek pure eternity in the form of primordiality, and to seek the witnessing of beauty, on the basis of the goal of paradise in the clothing of actions. Nothing of the world of the angelic realm was unveiled to me for an hour, and I was amazed about my condition. I saw the Truth (glory be to him) in the quality of his nearness to me, and I said to myself, "Where am I, if the Truth (glory be to him) is with me?" I saw him repeatedly in the form of majesty and beauty in all the regions of existence. It happened that I saw myself above Mount Sinai, and I saw the Truth (glory be to him) in the gardens of pre-eternity. It was as though he was scattering red and white roses, pearls and jewels. Moses, Abraham, and Muhammad with the chosen cherubs were crying out, wandering about, acting strangely, and laughing. Some were in astonishment, some in joy and rejoicing. They were in the state of flight from the assaults of power. Then I saw the Truth (glory be to him), and before him was a river flowing with wine. He gave me to drink, and spoke to me words—if these were spoken to deaf rocks, they would fly from joy. He called me by name repeatedly, and he called me and confided in me and clothed me in the clothing of loveliness and glory, until I fell with the people of the angelic realm, witnessing, witnessed, beloved. Then he was kind to me, and hid from me.

❀ 205. By the Kaʿba

Time passed, and I saw the Most High, above the ladders of the world of the throne, and above the throne. I saw him in the world of pre-eternity in the form of isolation. Then time passed, and he called me near, and I answered him repeatedly. Then I saw myself in the sanctuary of the Kaʿba, and the Truth (glory be to him) manifested himself in the interior of the Kaʿba in the form of beauty, glory, and majesty. The Prophet was there with the prophets and the angels, turning around the Kaʿba. I saw the throne as though it descended and walked around the Kaʿba. I found from the Truth that which I found, and I heard what I heard; I cannot reveal these secrets, for they are from the sciences of the unknown, which issue from the chosen attributes and chosen actions. They are only known to knowers of God who have drunk the oceans of oneness and have known the Truth by the impressions of unknowings, and the sanctification of attributes and the essence beyond the thoughts of the hearts of humanity, from the throne to the earth. God transcends every imagining that is incommensurate with his power.

❀ 206. Pretenders and Politics

It happened that I stopped with a group of people with claims [to spiritual status], but their demands were without substance. I was distressed by their demands when I saw that their claims were the frivolities of humanity. A group urged me to see the ruler [Takala ibn Zangi], an experience that was very intense and difficult for me, because of having to go among them. I was very worried; inwardly I was near misery. I slept there, and my sleep was the sleep of reclining. I awoke at midnight, and that was on a Wednesday in the month of Sha‘ban in the year 85 [585 hijri, or September 1189]. I was in danger of falling asleep, and God came to me, saying, "They wish to extinguish the light of God with their mouths, but God refuses, except that he will perfect his light, though the unbelievers hate it" [Qur’an 9:32]. And that conversation took place while my bodily nature was rising from the spell of sleep.

❀ 207. The Form of Greatness

I sat and did ablutions and prayed two cycles. I was in extreme distress. Then I undertook the task of remembering the names of God most high, because of my distress on his account. But I did not encounter the sweetness of that utterance. And when I finished these two cycles and the prayer following that, I awaited the opening of the doors of the hidden. I saw the Truth (glory be to him) near to me, and he unveiled to me beauty, the beauty of his transcendent face, and one of the attributes of his glory, with the attributes of greatness. Now in greatness there is shock and assault, but between me and the Truth there is distance without extension. He said to me, "Why are you concerned, when I am yours in the form of greatness?" A visitation of ecstasy assaulted me, which would have melted all the mountains of the world. Then I saw him, then I saw him, then I saw him, more times than I can count. Then the lights of his attributes shone out from every region in the eclipse of his attributes and his essence. Then he showed his transcendent self to me in the form of the descent from sublime knowledge, and the beyond the beyond, on the highland of greatness, and his greatness filled the throne, the footstool, the heavens, and earth.

✤ 208. Arrayed in the Form of Divinity

He guided me through the greatest angelic realm, and he unveiled to me the wombs of eternity and the bellies of pre-eternity in the form of transcendence, loveliness, and majesty. Then he appeared to me arrayed in one of the forms of divinity. All the cherubs were at the front of the pavilions of his greatness, on the threshold of loveliness and beauty; they had tresses like the tresses of women and houris, in the clothes of the people of the garden of paradise, separating and gathering. I saw Gabriel in the form of loveliness and beauty, which I cannot describe; he passed by me in his loveliness and beauty. I saw the prophets and saints drowned in the lights of the sublimities of his majesty. I was between veiling and manifestation, I was fainting, wild, crying out, weeping, longing, raving like a drunkard. All my worries and sorrows departed, and my heart was filled with happiness in his intimacy and beauty.

✤ 209. Plague and Politics

After that I prayed, and I interceded with God most high for the people of Muhammad. That was during a time when in Shiraz there was a great epidemic, death, illnesses, and dropsy. Then I asked God most high that he free me from entering the courts of princes. After dawn, one of God's orders (glory be to him) came down, and he freed me from seeing them or associating with them at that time. God is transcendent, I have hope from him, and by his grace he makes me independent of any other than him. I seek his aid, and he is sufficient for me.

✤ 210. Colophon

The book *The Unveiling of Secrets* was completed with the aid of God, and praise belongs to God in every state.

INDICES

Index 1

Sections of *The Unveiling of Secrets* Discussed in *Ruzbihan Baqli: Mysticism and the Rhetoric of Sainthood in Persian Sufism*

Qur'anic Passages

Sayings of the Prophet Muhammad

ties indicated by the names of God, passim

Azraʾil: angel of death, 23, 93, 122

Bayazid al-Bistami, *see* Abu Yazid al-Bistami

beauty *(jamal):* divine qualities of loveliness and grace that evoke love, passim

bees, 114

bewilderment *(hayaman):* an advanced stage of love that halts thought, 11, 16, 37, 78, 86, 105, 110, 121, 128, 129, 130, 134

birds, 41, 59, 84, 88, 112

Bistami, *see* Abu Yazid al-Bistami

Black Stone: the stone set in one corner of the Kaʿba, 34

blood, 19, 41, 49, 90, 103, 108, 119

books, 8, 37, 47, 95, 141

bows, 57, 62, 63, 84, 86, 93

bread, 15

brides, 6, 43, 47, 48, 59, 69, 72, 88, 91, 95

brocade, 41

butterflies, 86

caliphs: successors to the Prophet Muhammad, 14, 31, 32

camels, 28, 29, 36

candles, 106

carnal soul *(nafs),* 34

carpets, 26, 50, 59

castles, 13, 14, 18, 54, 61, 111, 112

catapult, 113

chants, 108

cherubs *(karrubiyyun):* powerful angels, 71, 74, 79, 91, 115, 133, 135, 138, 141

children, 9, 48, 54, 61, 126, 133

city, 63

cloaks, 18, 29, 42, 118, 126, 127

clothed with divinity *(iltibas),* xix, 6, 18, 29, 42, 48, 50, 55, 68, 70, 72, 78, 94, 95, 97, 98, 99, 111, 116, 118, 122, 126, 128, 141

companions, 81, 87, 88, 127, 135

conscience or consciousness *(sirr):* inner faculty of awareness, xii, passim; *see also* secret

Corbin, Henry, xx

crow, 100

cycles *(rukʿa)* of ritual prayer, 27, 62, 79, 82, 100, 114, 140

dance, 34, 64, 74, 106

dates, 19

daughters, 112

David, 21, 109

death, 23, 29, 68, 121, 122, 141

descent *(nuzul),* of angels, 91, 95; of God, 18, 22, 28, 30, 49, 50, 69, 76, 78, 117, 140; of prophets, 18, 47; of Ruzbihan, 94; of states, 65, 70, 112, 113

Dhu al-Nun al-Misri (d. 859): early Sufi of Egypt, 127

discipline *(riyada):* meditative exercise, 108

ditches, 19, 103

diving, 5, 10, 89, 94, 100, 123

divine presence *(baqaʾ):* the experience of God's reality after human consciousness has been obliterated, xix, 8, 15, 18, 20, 29, 36, 60, 63, 69, 77, 81, 84, 87, 94, 98, 108, 126, 129, 131, 132, 133, 134, 137, 138

dog, 92

door, 35

dove, 36

dream, 33, 97

drinking, 14, 18, 21, 52, 68, 75, 84, 137, 139; tears, 92, 93; wine, 20, 23, 24, 31, 106, 114, 119, 130

drums, 71, 91, 95, 127

drunkards, 6, 9, 31, 47, 66, 68, 74, 110, 141

dust, 66, 102, 116

East, 14, 21, 69, 86, 92, 124, 125

ecstasy *(wajd),* passim

Eden, 54

Jaʿfar al-Hadhdhaʾ (d. 952): early Persian Sufi, 89

Jamal al-Din Abi al-Wafaʾ ibn Khalil al-Fasaʾi (twelfth cent.): a Sufi who was companion and teacher to Ruzbihan, 12

Jesus, 18, 21, 29, 31, 32, 93, 136

jewels, 17, 18, 62, 76, 113, 116, 135, 138

jinn, 27, 51

John the Baptist, 80

Joseph, 43, 79, 80, 97, 109, 130

Junayd (d. 910): famous early Sufi of Baghdad, 81, 106, 127

jurists (fuqahaʾ), 83

Kaʿba: the sacred shrine of Muslims at Mecca, built by Abraham and Ismaʿil, 33, 34, 35, 139

Khidr: deathless prophet who instructed Moses, 14, 115, 121, 138

Khurasan: northeast Persia, 28

king, 17, 43

kingdom, 4, 6, 18, 35, 37, 51, 64, 65, 85, 105, 109, 116, 119, 129

laughter, 17, 45, 46, 71, 73, 91, 95, 111, 138

law, 6

likeness, 4, 19, 22, 43, 46, 47, 57, 59, 61, 73, 77, 80, 85, 98, 107, 110, 117, 119, 120, 123, 128

lion, 9, 41, 121

Little Bear (the constellation Ursa Minor), xiv, 15, 16, 56

lodge (ribat): residence or hospice for Sufis, 11, 27, 28, 68, 70, 71, 74, 90

lordship (rububiyya): divine dominion, 94, 99, 128, 129

lotus, 64

love (mahabba): the many-leveled attraction toward divine beauty, passim

lute, 23, 71, 81, 118, 127, 132

madman, 59, 127

majesty (jalal): divine qualities of authority and power that engender awe, passim

Malik: the angel in charge of hell, 69

Malik ibn Anas (d. 795): imam or founder of the Maliki school of law, 135

manifestation (tajalli): theophany or appearance of divine reality in perceptible form, passim

martyrs, 24, 35

Maʿruf Karkhi (d. 815): early Sufi of Baghdad, 127

Massignon, Louis, xx

masters (shaykh), 65, 74, 81, 85, 89, 92, 95, 106, 108, 109, 113, 121, 127, 135

Mecca, 33, 35

Medina, 56

meditation (muraqaba), 4, 10, 25, 41, 43, 49, 53, 59, 72, 74, 79, 99, 100, 104, 117, 128

melons, 18

Michael: one of the chief angels, 23, 31, 93, 122

might (jabarut): the realm where apparitions of divine power are experienced, 5, 13, 18, 37, 41, 44, 48, 51, 53, 57, 63, 69, 81, 82, 85, 97, 102, 109, 112, 119, 121, 123

mines, 58, 73

miracles, 87, 88, 97, 123, 124

mirror, 4, 47, 88, 130

moon, 20, 46, 47, 81, 117

Moses, 18, 29, 31, 32, 50, 51, 60, 80, 93, 94, 97, 101, 113, 136, 138; descending Sinai, 22, 47, 92; in God's presence, 7, 98, 102, 123, 130, 137

mosque, 9

moth, 101

mother, 48, 53, 61, 126

Mount, see Greatness; Qaf; Sinai

mountains, 8, 11, 14, 27, 47, 50, 56, 68, 77, 92, 107, 126, 133, 140

Muhammad the Prophet (d. 632), 5, 10, 71, 80, ascension of, 7, 64, 98, 141;

Ridwan: the angel who guards paradise, 18, 35, 54, 91

rivers, 4, 57, 61, 66, 111, 115, 132, 139

rolling, 102, 121

roof, 11, 13, 15, 68, 71, 74, 90

roses, passim

rubies, 24

Rumi (d. 1277), ix

ruse, 52

Ruwaym (d. 915): early Persian Sufi, 81, 106

Ruzbihan Baqli (d. 1209), passim; addressed by name, 13, 25, 28, 32, 34, 50, 61, 62, 85

sacrificial victims, 104

Safaʾ: a hill near Mecca, 34

sainthood *(wilaya)*, 4, 7, 13, 32, 101

saints *(awliyaʾ, pl. of wali):* those who are close to God and are granted authority by him, 4, 5, 6, 20, 21, 24, 25, 27, 35, 36, 37, 41, 56, 61, 71, 76, 83, 85, 88, 90, 93, 97, 99, 113, 117, 121, 122, 123, 135, 138, 141

Salih: ancient Arabian prophet, 29

sand, 35

sapphires, 24, 56

Sari al-Saqati (d. 867): early Sufi, 57, 127

Satan, 123

satanic imaginings, 128

satisfaction *(ridaʾ):* divine acceptance, 18, 25, 44, 46, 55, 66, 76, 132, 134, 135

scholars *(ʿulamaʾ),* 83

secret *(sirr):* inner faculty of awareness, xii, 3, 5, 6, 9, 30, 32, 44, 55, 58, 59, 63, 68, 70, 75, 80, 87, 105, 114, 124, 125, 128, 130, 131, 139, 141

self-blaming *(malamati),* 22

servanthood *(ʿubudiyya):* the condition of the created with respect to God, 94, 110, 128

seventy thousand: cosmic number signifying totality, 16, 22, 31, 60, 62, 70, 75, 85, 98, 108, 109

Shaʿban: eighth month of Islamic lunar calendar, 140

Shafiʿi (d. 820): imam or founder of the Shafiʿi legal school, to which Ruzbihan belonged, 83, 135

shaykhs: Sufi masters, 10, 12, 15, 22, 27, 28, 29, 47, 74, 89, 106

shepherd, 23

Shiraz, 65, 68, 70, 85, 90, 138, 141

shrouds, 23

silk, 47, 57, 89

Sinai, 22, 50, 92, 94, 138

sincere ones *(siddiqun):* the highest rank of perfect saints, 4, 6, 7, 70, 79, 91, 92, 93, 109, 114, 120, 133

singers, 100, 122

slander, 92

sleep, 17, 62, 76, 98, 116, 130, 134, 137, 140

snakes, 57

snow, 30, 47, 115

sobriety *(sahw),* 6, 44, 63, 64, 68, 88, 108, 110

soldiers, 36

Solomon, 109

sons, 58, 75, 98, 112, 136, 137

space, 4, 14, 19, 43, 65, 66, 88, 98, 102, 108, 110

spear, 86

speech, 4, 6, 28, 34, 45, 67, 76, 78, 93, 104, 133

spindle, 23

spirit *(ruh),* passim

stars, 4, 16, 47, 56, 81

states *(ahwal, pl. of hal):* the onset of spiritual experiences as divine gifts, 6, 8, 11, 12, 15, 19, 36, 45, 53, 64, 65, 66, 71, 72, 73, 85, 88, 90, 109, 113, 115, 118, 124, 137

station *(maqam):* a stage in the spiritual path traversed by the mystic, passim

stones, 4, 8, 113

striving *(mujahada):* ascetic practices, 6, 11, 37, 108, 121

Substitutes *(abdal, pl. of badal):*